Essays on the ODYSSEY

Essays on the ODYSSEY

Selected Modern Criticism

Edited by

CHARLES H. TAYLOR, JR.

INDIANA UNIVERSITY PRESS
Bloomington & London

FOURTH PRINTING 1967

Manufactured in the United States of America
Library of Congress catalog card number: 63-9722

Contents

Introduction

HOMER's *Odyssey* is more widely read today than any other classic of Greek literature. The account of Odysseus' struggle to return home and to regain his kingdom following the Trojan War appeals at once to nearly every reader, however unfamiliar he may be with the conventions of epic poetry and the traditions of Greek culture. Indeed, the poem is widely taught in American colleges and universities because it is such a successful introduction to these conventions and traditions.

I believe it will be useful to both students and teachers to have in one volume a selection of essays which explore from modern critical points of view the meaning of the *Odyssey*. The number of essays included is deliberately limited so that the collection can be readily available to any interested reader. The volume is meant not to be comprehensive in scope but rather stimulating in content, posing various interpretations of the poem which illuminate several of its many themes. Although we know today that the *Iliad* and the *Odyssey* are the products of long oral traditions and may or may not have been shaped in their final form by the same man, the impact of each poem on our culture, as on Greek culture, has been as a coherent and meaningful whole. I have, therefore, included only essays which assume the essential integrity of the *Odyssey* as a work of art.

The range of perspectives from which the poem is viewed produces sometimes essentially incompatible readings. These disagreements derive not only from the different angles of vision from which the critics see the poem, but also from the extraordinary richness of the character of Odysseus. A reading will vary considerably with the traits or episodes the critic chooses to emphasize in his treatment of the poem. While there is no such thing as a perfectly balanced reading, I would hope that there is sufficient variety here to foster careful thought on the values which give the poem its life. Those who are interested in developing a wider acquaintance with the large body of Homeric scholarship will find the notes to some of the essays, gathered together at the end of the volume, a useful guide.

The seven essays included are arranged in the order of their publication, the final one by Anne Amory being printed for the first time in this collection. The others are reprinted from the books or periodicals in which they originally appeared at various times during the last decade. I am most grateful to the author and the publisher of each essay for permission to reprint it; the specific source of each piece is cited at the beginning of the essay.

The arrangement of the essays in chronological order of publication reveals the extent to which some of the pieces either build on or respond to their predecessors. Moreover, in reading the essays through in the order in which they appeared, there is discernible an increasing interest in what might be called the emblematic or symbolic implications of the events and images of the poem.

The first essay, "Gods and Men in Homer" by W. K. C. Guthrie, is the only one which does not focus primarily on the *Odyssey;* I have included it because the distinctions Professor Guthrie draws are fundamental to a sound understanding both of the *Odyssey* itself and of the assumptions made by the other critics when they treat the relations between divine and human characters in the poem.

W. B. Stanford's "Personal Relationships" provides a sensitive review of the panorama of interesting figures, both natural and supernatural, whom Odysseus confronts in his travels and on his return to Ithaca. His survey of the interaction of Odysseus with these diverse individuals leads him to interesting observations about the character of the hero and he touches upon many aspects of the poem which are dealt with from other perspectives in subsequent essays.

In "The *Odyssey* and the Western World" George deF. Lord views the poem as an integral part of the epic tradition in which the hero has a duty to his society. He presents a vigorously argued case for Odysseus as a hero in need of rehabilitation before his return to Ithaca. Through his experiences on his return from Troy, Lord maintains, Odysseus is recivilized and prepared to undertake the responsibilities of his kingdom.

George E. Dimock, Jr., on the other hand, holds in "The Name of Odysseus" that Odysseus' only obligation, in terms of the values of the poem, is to live up to his name. This, Dimock suggests, means "trouble," not only for others, but for himself as well. It is the duty of the hero, as his adventures show, to achieve a unique and enduring identity without regard to the welfare of others than himself.

William S. Anderson in "Calpyso and Elysium" concerns himself primarily with the meaning for the definition of the hero of two juxtaposed worlds: the Elysium promised to Menelaus (which is previewed in the rich ennui of Sparta) and the analogous image of Calypso's Ogygia which is presented in the following book. An end such as distinguishes Menelaus is rejected by Odysseus, from which we learn much about the essential nature of the hero.

In "The Obstacles to Odysseus' Return" I point to the underlying similarities between Odysseus' diverse opponents and temptations. These constitute a panoply of closely related forces working against Odysseus and representing those instinctual and chthonic powers in human experience which are the enemies of conscious selfhood. Indirectly, I also suggest a concept of the hero's character and ends which falls between the conflicting views of Lord and Dimock.

Appropriately, the final essay, Anne Amory's "The Reunion of Odysseus and Penelope," is concerned with the end of the poem. It presents a sensitive study of Penelope's relations with Odysseus after he enters his palace and before he is fully acknowledged. Approaching their reunion as a part of a larger study of dreams and omens in the poem, Mrs. Amory explores Penelope's growing awareness that Odysseus has returned. She shows that her responses, though complex, are understandably feminine.

Each of the seven essays suggests in its own terms some of the reasons for the *Odyssey's* extraordinarily durable appeal. Together, they should send the reader back to the poem with a heightened awareness of its significance.

CHARLES H. TAYLOR, JR.

Yale University
August, 1962

I

Gods and Men in Homer

W. K. C. GUTHRIE

ἐξ ἀρχῆς καθ' Ὅμηρον ἐπεὶ μεμεθήκασι πάντες.

Since all men's thoughts have been shaped by Homer from the beginning.

XENOPHANES

"To THE Homeric Greeks the state was not yet the centre of life. . . . On the other hand, Homer not only provided the foundation on which the Polis and the people of the Polis stood; he was their companion, always present to them, always alive with them, exerting a continuous and strong influence upon them."[1]

With these words no one could well disagree, and they must be my excuse for saying something on an already overworked subject about which I have little or nothing that is new to offer. So great was the authority of Homer that much in later Greek belief is either in fact a development of Homeric teaching[2] or was believed to be so by the Greeks. The latter circumstance is not irrelevant, since it meant that the reasons for following a certain religious practice, that is, the

---

Reprinted by permission from *The Greeks and Their Gods,* The Beacon Press, Boston, 1950, chapter four. Copyright 1950 by Methuen & Co., Ltd.

To understand this essay fully, it is helpful to have in mind the distinction Professor Guthrie makes between divine being and human being in the concluding paragraph of the preceding chapter:

". . . We shall treat the concepts *god* or *divinity* and *immortal* as equivalents, because they were so for the Greeks. Gods may have other characteristics, but primarily and essentially they are the immortals, and it is their immortality which differentiates them from men. To say *gods* and

current belief behind it, might suffer considerable distortion in Greek minds owing to their sincere belief that it was not contrary to anything in Homer and their desire to respect his authority, although in fact the practice in question might have its origin in a different world from Homer's and have sprung from feelings incompatible with those of his heroes. It is true therefore, even though in a somewhat peculiar sense, that a great deal in later Greek religion is only a development of Homeric ideas. Owing to the existence of other strong influences, the development might go so far that the last stage was radically different from the first, but even so it rarely happened that all traces of Homeric origin were lost. Often it is that which gives the key to something which would otherwise seem a curious and inconsequent series of ideas. It is true in the sense that the Greeks believed themselves to be following Homer and in that belief modified considerably certain parts of their religious inheritance from other sources. I shall suggest later that the Eleusinian mysteries show a striking example of this adaptation in the beliefs held about the different fates which awaited the souls of the initiated and the uninitiated.[3]

Our theme, then, demands some reference to the relations between gods and men in Homer, but the familiarity of Homeric religion may allow us to deal with it shortly. Professor Rose has shown convincingly that the key to its understanding lies in the organization of

---

men, the Greek might use the words *theoi* and *anthropoi,* but he might equally well use the words *athanatoi* and *thnetoi. Athanatos* (immortal) is an adjective, and may therefore be used in conjunction with *theos.* But it may equally well stand alone, and its meaning then is unambiguous: it means *god* and nothing else, just as *theos* does. It follows that to believe the soul to be immortal is to believe it to be divine. If man is immortal, then he is god. This is universal in Greek, and it is perhaps worth while drawing attention to it, seeing that we ourselves think differently. We also discuss the immortality of the soul. Some believe in it and some do not. But neither side is accustomed to regard the question as one of equating man with god. To the Greek the two were indissolubly bound together. Yet in glibly asking the question 'Did the Greeks believe in the immortality of the soul?' we are apt to forget the peculiar difficulties with which such a conception was for them bound up. To believe in the immortality of the soul was the same as saying: 'Man is a kind of god.' There were indeed Greeks who did not shrink from saying that, but let us first of all be clear in our minds about all that was involved in the statement."

Homeric society. It is of course the religion of the chieftains and heroes which we learn of in the poems. Little or nothing is said of the religion of common people, which may have been very different. In the eyes of the warlike aristocracy gods and men together formed one society, organized on a basis of strongly marked class-distinctions as was the human society itself. The highest class of aristocrats were the gods, their relation to the whole of mankind is much the same as that of the king or chieftain (*basileus*) to the lower orders, and the analogy between the two—*basileis* and gods—is helpful in considering questions of mutual relationships and obligations, and of morality.[4]

That gods and goddesses were thought of in this way, as Agamemnon or Achilles, Helen or Arete raised to an even higher degree, brings them in one way closer to mankind, but in another way emphasizes the distance between them. They are closer to mankind in character. Certain faults are unsuited to the nobility, mainly because they detract from its dignity, but from all faults they are certainly not expected to be free. It is the same with the gods. They have a certain, though by our standards a rather crude, code of conduct. On the whole they will be expected to deal fairly, since petty fraud at least is beneath their dignity, but they will not hesitate to stoop to unfairness or deceit on occasion if it suits their purpose. Again, in the sphere of sexual morality, a person of the rank of Agamemnon or Achilles felt at liberty to take any woman whom he fancied from the lower orders. It was his right, as one of kingly line, and indeed to be thus singled out was to be regarded as an honor by the recipient of his favors. There was certainly no stain on the character of either. The loves of gods for mortals form a parallel to this. Cruelty, provided again it be not too petty, is thought little of, either in the dealings of one of the kings with the people under his sway or in the behavior of the gods towards their subjects, mankind as a whole. It is quite natural for Menelaos to speak of "clearing out a city" for Odysseus when he offers him a home in the Peloponnese. No one would question his right to do so, nor would they question any more the right of a god to act as he pleased towards men.[5] Since however the society was a courtly one, showing in fact a strong resemblance to the knightly chivalry of the Middle Ages, we find that side by side with cruelty or caprice in action goes a marked preference for the *suaviter in modo*. This does not indeed hold good, any more than it held good in medieval chivalry, between the upper class and the common men, but just as the *basileis* expected it from each other (save in exceptional outbursts of uncontrollable temper), so they had quite a high enough opinion of their own standing to expect it from the gods, for in spite of the difference of level they belonged to the same aristocratic circle. The conversation between Achilles and Athene at the beginning of the *Iliad* is instructive.[6] In his anger against Agamemnon Achilles was drawing his sword from its scabbard to strike him down, when Athene appeared, at Hera's bidding, to see that these two heroes did each other no harm. She stood behind him and took him by his fair hair, appearing to him alone. Achilles turned round in astonishment and recognized her at once, and he was the first to speak, asking her why she had come. Was it to witness the insolence of Agamemnon? "Then let me tell you," he went on, "that his arrogance will soon cost him his life." And the goddess replies, "I came to turn aside your wrath, if you will hearken to me," and goes on to promise him a threefold reward of rich gifts if he will put up with Agamemnon's provocation now. "I must needs respect your word and Hera's," answers Achilles, "bitter though my anger be. It is better thus. He who obeys the gods is hearkened to by them."

"If you will hearken to me," says Athene, and the hero replies that he will, for he knows it is better to do so, and if he does he may hope for something from the gods in return. He speaks as a free agent, almost as an equal, and the courtesies are preserved throughout. It may have been a polite fiction, for there was indeed little hope for one who set himself up against an immortal god, unless his case caused a split in the ranks of the immortals themselves so that he had a more powerful god on his side. Zeus' thunderbolts or the storms of Poseidon were weapons which no mortal could counter, but for the most part they were in the background and it was not good form to mention them in a conversation between a god and a man.

Gods, then, come near to men in having a moral character beset by many of the same frailties. In another way too they appear simply as the highest stratum of one complex society—and this no doubt goes far to account for the courtesies of intercourse and the fiction of equality which we have noticed—namely that men may be related to them by blood. The gods were captivated by mortal beauty. They mated with fair women and had offspring, and these offspring were the kings among men, with the titles "god-born" or "god-nurtured." Of the royal pair in Phaeacia, Alcinous was the grandson of Poseidon, and Arete his great-granddaughter; Achilles was the son of an immortal mother, the sea-goddess Thetis, by a mortal father; and so forth. Yet the children of these mixed marriages remained mortal. They had blood, not ichor, in their veins. Curiously enough, this conception of the gods, linking them morally and physically so closely to mankind, is the one which bars the way most effectively to any aspirations after divinity in man. It emphasizes rather than blurs the absolute division between the *thneton* and the *athanaton.* A more spiritual notion of divinity, such as later came to the surface in Greek religion, may make the division more shadowy, and hold out hopes of a different sort of relationship whose consummation is the merging of the two together.

There is no hint of this in Homer, nor is the reason far to seek. What made the gods approach our level was an element of human nature in them, not a hint of the divine in us. The parallel between god and earthly *basileus* holds good. Morally the kings or barons may share their failings with the lower orders, but in any matter affecting their prestige it goes ill with the unlucky being who tries to set himself up against them or do them any hurt. Treason, or disloyalty to the lord, is the unforgivable crime. Only one person in Homer is represented as being tortured. It is the serf Melanthius, the goatherd, because he tried to betray Odysseus his master, and the fate of the women of Penelope's household, who had committed the same offence against their lord, is likewise unparalleled.[7] Similarly when men are punished by the gods, it is not usually on moral grounds, because they have sinned in our sense of the word. They are punished for personal offences against the gods. The few who are condemned to eternal torment—Ixion, Tityos, Tantalus, Sisyphus—had personally affronted Zeus. Ixion had assaulted Hera. The only immorality involved was an infringement of Zeus' prerogative. The offence of Sisyphus was actually to have given away the secret of one of Zeus' own intrigues.[8] The myth of Prometheus, though first told for us in Hesiod, is an outstanding example of the same motive for divine punishment. His crime was that he tried to place in the hands of men powers which had been reserved for the gods. The resentment of Zeus was aroused because he feared for the continuance of his tyranny.

As the story of Sisyphus shows, it is not for men to criticize or interfere with the actions of the gods, be they good or bad. The gods may criticize each other, and do so freely. Similarly Achilles may tell Agamemnon his opinion of him in no measured terms; but let Thersites, one of lower rank, try to do the same, and his ears are ignominiously boxed. It is not suggested that Agamemnon did not deserve the criticism, but it was not for such as Thersites to give it.

It is in this matter of rank, prestige and power that gods and men are so sharply divided. Herodotus makes Solon say: "I know that deity is full of envy and unstableness,"[9] and the words carry no suggestion of impiety. They are a statement of a fact that was generally recognized. The surest way to arouse the jealousy of the gods was μὴ θνητὰ φρονεῖν, to forget your mortality. In this unbridgeable gulf between the mortal and the immortal lay the difference which gave the gods the right to act as cruelly and capriciously as they cared. They are the "easy livers" (ῥεῖα ζώοντες) who never know death. Man is the creature of a season. It is in Homer that we first meet that pathetic simile to describe his ephemeral nature, which found such a ready echo in the elegiac poets of Ionia: "Even as are the generations of leaves, so also are those of men. The leaves of this year the wind strows upon the earth, but the forest burgeoneth and putteth forth more. So of the generations of men one putteth forth and another ceaseth."[10] The attitude of the Homeric heroes to the possibility of a future life was one of complete pessimism. They were wealthy aristocrats who had won their position by physical prowess. The body was the source of their joy in life, for they had a full and zestful appreciation of its pleasures—sport, meat and drink, and love—and most of their life was spent in the enjoyment of these, or in war which was the means whereby they secured them. Consequently a robust physical frame was the *sine qua non* of happiness. Old age was a grievous evil no less than death, which in their eyes was the separation of the life of man, his *psyche,* from the body. It was not extinction, but meant dragging on an existence deprived of all that made life worth living. Hence the Homeric conception of the dead as strengthless, miserable wraiths, and hence the outburst of Achilles to Odysseus that he would rather be a laborer working for a poor man on earth than rule as a king among the dead.[11] It is safe to say that this statement was based on very little knowledge of what the life of a poor man's servant on earth was like.

This view of the Homeric gods, which explains their nature by an analogy, drawn in the minds of their worshippers, with the contemporary pattern of an earthly ruler, is shared by Nilsson, who writes that the model of the Homeric pantheon "is found solely in the feudal Mycenean kingship of which Homer has preserved traces easily recognizable," and that "the divine community is a copy of the conditions of the age of chivalry."[12] Whereas however we have here, following Rose, used this analogy to account in particular for their peculiar moral character, and the way in which, in their relations with mankind, most of the emphasis is laid on power and little on righteousness or justice, Nilsson on this point adopts a different explanation. He prefers to account for it as something left over from their origin as nature-spirits. "Of all the numerous characteristics which the gods carried with them from their primitive origin on their journey towards a higher religious plane, characteristics to which the Homeric anthropomorphism gave such clearness and prominence, none was more fateful than the lack of any connexion with morality. . . . The power of the gods, and not its limitations, was present to the religious consciousness. The absence of morality preyed on the vital nerve of religious feeling. In proportion as the gods are Nature-gods, they have nothing to do with morals. The rain falls alike upon the just and the unjust. Animism implants in the gods human will and feeling, passions and caprices."[13] The contrast between the two explanations is instructive (and this is why I have thought it worth while to quote them both) because of their difference in kind. One scholar seeks to explain a phenomenon of a certain age by reference to a remote and misty past, whose reconstruction depends to a large extent on inference and analogy, the other relies on known characteristics of contemporary thought and society. My own preference should be clear by now, and perhaps a little more may be said in justification of it.

In Homer the will of a great man is his law. He does not so much do things because they are right. Rather, since he is an irresponsible aristocrat, they are right because he does them.[14] This can be illustrated very simply by the change in meaning undergone by one of the commonest of Greek words, the word *dike*. We translate it "justice," and something akin to that meaning it acquired very early. But whether or not its etymology connects it, as is probable, with the meaning "direction" or "way," the earliest sense of which we have record is that of the "customary behavior" of any particular class. In this sense it is commonly used with a dependent genitive. This first example shows how far removed it was in the mind of the writer from any sense of "justice." The men of Ithaca have forgotten, complains Penelope, during the long absence of Odysseus, what an unusual king he was. "He never did nor said anything unfair among the people, though that is the *dike* (the usual way) of god-like kings: one man will they hate, and favor another." In the following we may be sure that the meaning intended was the same, though they show how easily the word could slip from signifying no more than what was customary to indicating what was right and just. [Eumaeus the swineherd to Odysseus:] "What I have to give is little, though gladly given; for that is the *dike* of (the way with) servants, who live in constant fear when young men are their lords." [The mother of Odysseus, when he tries to embrace her and finds that she is a mere bodiless shade:] "Nay this is the *dike* of (what happens to) mortals, when one of us dies." [Odysseus, in disguise, to Penelope, who has asked him who he is:] "Thou layest upon me fresh grief in addition to that which I already bear: for that is *dike* (for so it is) when a man is parted from his homeland so long as I now have been." A pleasant example is furnished by the meeting of Odysseus with his old father, whom he finds working in the fields like a common laborer. Odysseus congratulates him on his husbandry but suggests that he does not look the sort of man who should be doing this work. He should rather be in a position to enjoy his bath and his meal and then go comfortably off to sleep. "For that is the *dike* of old men." Here the word may indicate a habit or a right. No doubt Odysseus had both in mind and *dike* can easily mean both together.[15]

Justice, then, for the Greeks consisted first of all in doing what custom alone had established as being suitable for a particular station in life, whether that of serf (*dmos*), king or even god. The gods, however, being the highest class, are also the most free. The slave does not dictate to his lord, nor a mortal to a god. The king dictates to his people, and gods to men. Hence *dike* for us is what the gods will. It is right because they will it, not vice versa. Nevertheless, as we have observed, one cannot help having a certain idea of how a king ought to behave. Neither cruelty nor a hot temper nor a roving eye for women is outside the *dike* of king or god, but certain types of baseness or pettiness are. It can hardly be called a high conception of divine morality, but it contained the seeds of an ethical religion. The word *dike* itself early acquired the thoroughly moral coloring which it has in Aeschylus, and when Euripides makes a character cry, "If the gods do aught ugly,[16] they are no gods!" he could easily have maintained that his teaching was only that of Homer, who sang of gods who acted according to *dike*. If it seems important to make it clear that Homer and Euripides had different qualities in mind, it is no less important to understand how easy it was for a Greek to ignore the distinction. Both would profess their belief that the gods, if true gods, must follow *dike,* and though we may be aware that the word had radically changed its meaning, this cannot have been so obvious to those who used it.

It is not of course true that the only meaning of *dike* in Homer is what I have called the earlier one, and that all moral developments of the word must be sought in post-Homeric literature. This is perhaps a good place to remind ourselves of the inadequacy of throwing (as Wilamowitz put it) everything Homeric into the same pot. His reasoning was that if one passage seemed to show a more advanced morality than another, then that passage was later, and in this and other ways the great poems were chopped up. It is possible to be grateful to him for drawing our attention to the differences without following him in his explanation of their origin. Without denying that there are earlier and later elements in the Homeric poems, we may doubt whether this matter of moral "advance" provides a satisfactory criterion for distinguishing them. Even the general belief that the *Odyssey* is a later poem than the *Iliad,* which is doubtless right, could be as easily refuted as supported by arguments drawn from the moral atmosphere. Wilamowitz quotes in one place the joyful cry of Laertes when Odysseus announces his victory: "There are still gods on Olympus, if the suitors have really paid the penalty for their *hybris*."[17] Anything like this, he says, would be unthinkable in the *Iliad*. Yet all my examples of the earlier, non-moral sense of *dike* have been drawn from the *Odyssey,* simply because they were easier to find there,[18] and there is a passage, admittedly unique, in the *Iliad* which depicts Zeus as eager to punish wrongdoing. It describes, for the purposes of a simile, how Zeus sends a storm on an autumn day. The whole black earth is oppressed by it, and Zeus pours down a furious rain, because "he is heavy with anger against men, who in the assembly pass crooked judgments by force, and drive out justice [*dike*], heeding not the vengeance of the gods."[19] Since the vengeance of Zeus here takes the form of showing his powers as a nature-god, the passage does not altogether support Nilsson's view, just quoted, that "in proportion as the gods are nature-gods, they have nothing to do with morals." This criticism surely has force, even if it be right to say, as he does, that the passage "occurs in a simile and therefore in one of the newest parts."[20] We need not go into the vexed question of early and late elements in Homer, for if our interpretation of the divine morality is right, chronological considerations have little to do with it, and I have tried to show that they break down when applied to it. It is in fact perfectly possible for the various conceptions of right that we have mentioned to coexist in the same society at the same time, and their coexistence is very naturally explained in the way here suggested, namely by supposing that to the people of whom Homer wrote the analogy between their kings and their gods was a close one. This needs no lengthy repetition. In general the will of a king, or a god, is his law. Neither is above human passions, they indulge in jealousy and favoritism and sometimes use dubious means to secure the safety of their favorites. Yet they uphold the chivalrous code of their society, which includes for example the duty of hospitality and the sanctity of the oath, and there will always be certain things which are outside their *dike* on grounds of *noblesse oblige*. Once the notion of obligation is introduced, however, its extension is easy and inevitable, and will vary according to individual preference. If the Homeric gods exhibit a mixture, to us almost incomprehensible, of irresponsible power and crude moral ideas, there is no need to separate the passages which emphasize the one or the other and assign them to different periods. The mixture was there all the time, and only serves to strengthen their resemblance to the Homeric *basileus,* for in him alone is that peculiar combination repeated.[21]

II

Personal Relationships

W. B. STANFORD

THE *Iliad* says nothing of Odysseus' private life during the Trojan campaign. One sees Achilles in the privacy of his tent and alone on the seashore, Hector in affectionate conversation with his wife and son, and Paris in acrimonious dalliance with Helen. But all Odysseus' actions, speeches, and conversations take place in public—in the camp, on the battlefield, in the council chamber, on embassies. He does, it is true, converse alone with Diomedes on the Night Raid; but his remarks are strictly confined to military matters. There is no suggestion that either Diomedes or anyone else in the Greek camp at Troy was his intimate friend. There was no one, apparently, among his associates at Troy to whom he could open his heart and speak without suspicion or caution.[1] Achilles had his mother and Patroclus to comfort him in his troubles. Agamemnon and Menelaus shared the familiarity of brothers. But Odysseus kept his inner thoughts and feelings to himself. In the *Odyssey,* too, even among his shipmates Odysseus is a lonely figure, more like Captain Ahab in Melville's *Moby Dick* than the genial prince that the Ithacans had known before the war.[2]

Homer suggests no reason for confining his account of Odysseus' Iliadic career to public activities and official relationships. Perhaps he simply decided to reserve the more intimate aspects of Odysseus' personal relationships for the *Odyssey* purely as a matter of poetic economy. But there may have been a less mechanical reason. A marked degree of separateness, and often even of loneliness, is the common

Reprinted by permission from *The Ulysses Theme: A Study in the Adaptability of a Traditional Hero,* Basil Blackwell, Oxford, 1954, chapter four.

fate of those gifted like Odysseus with an abnormal degree of intelligence and subtlety. Friendship is naturally difficult with a person of this calibre. The razor-edge of his mind and speech, however well controlled, will be widely feared. The psychological ambiguities and complexities of his character will seem to offer no firm foundation for loyalty or confidence. The fact that he does not seem to suffer from any of the more amiable weaknesses of human nature will thwart feelings of sympathy and affection. His general efficiency and success in whatever he undertakes will give an impression of inhumanity and self-sufficiency. And when these qualities are tainted with a reputation for deceitfulness and trickery, the obstacles to any sincere friendship become almost insuperable. This may have been what Homer intended to indicate by Odysseus' aloofness among his associates at Troy and his companions at sea.

This intention would also explain why Odysseus' relations with his family in Ithaca, as well as with the Phaeacians, Calypso, and Circe, were, in contrast, so easy and genial. His family knew him well enough not to mistrust his subtlety; the Phaeacians did not know his common reputation until he had won their friendship and respect; the amorous goddesses, being divine like his patron Athene, had no reason to fear his wiles; and, besides, the element of competition, which was constantly present in his dealings with the honor-loving heroes at Troy and the gain-loving companions of his voyages, would not affect his associations with close relatives, strangers, and divinities.

Whatever the reason for Odysseus' complete lack of intimate relationships among his comrades at arms, Homer with characteristic deftness hints early in the *Iliad* that it was not due to any incapacity for affection on Odysseus' part. Twice[3] under stress of strong emotion (in rebuking Thersites and in expostulating against Agamemnon's outrageous charges) Odysseus speaks of himself, in a unique expression, as the father of Telemachus, as if this were the title nearest to his heart. Similarly his love of home is obliquely expressed in his speech to the Greek host after the discomfiture of Thersites. No wonder, he says, that there is some disaffection among them, "for any man who stays away even one month from his wife is grieved . . . and we have been away for nine years."[4] Here Odysseus speaks from his own heart, though with an admirable avoidance of egotism.

In contrast with Homer's silence on Odysseus' personal relation-

ships in the *Iliad,* one finds them revealed very fully and variously in the *Odyssey.* A striking feature is that so many of them are with women. The post-Homeric tradition emphasized different aspects of these relationships according as literary fashions changed. Within more recent times writers under the influence of the romantic revival have tended to dwell more on his adventures with Circe, Calypso, and Nausicaa, than on his affection for his wife, parents, and son, as later chapters will show. Some have thought fit to present him as a primeval Don Juan or a primitive Byron. Others, following the fashion of the last three decades, have portrayed him as a man obsessed with sordid eroticism. Scholars and moralists, though naturally less extravagant, have noticed apparent inconsistencies between Odysseus' love for Penelope and his relationships with the women he met on his Odyssean wanderings.[5] This involves problems of fundamental importance for the development of the whole tradition, and it will be well to consider them in the full Homeric perspective here.

Justice demands that Odysseus' liaisons with Circe and Calypso should, like his wiliness, be viewed in the light of the customs of his time. On the one hand the Heroic Age was strictly monogamous; and Homer generally portrays the relationships between husbands and wives as affectionate, honorable, and equal. He offers little precedent for such a subordination of wives to husbands as one finds in later Greek epochs. A wife had to be wooed and won by a formal courtship and generous gifts. After marriage the wife organized and ruled the household, the husband looked after the estate and public affairs. In society they conversed, argued, or agreed, as equals. Homer does not hesitate at times to present women as more perceptive and intelligent than men. Arete is cleverer than Alcinous, Helen than Menelaus, Clytaemnestra (in a brutal way) than Agamemnon. In fact there have been few periods of European literature when women have been portrayed with such a frank appraisal as in the *Iliad* and *Odyssey.* Homer presents them without adulation or contempt, without romanticism or mysticism, simply as another kind of human being who is in some ways stronger and in some ways weaker than men.

On the other hand women suffered from one grave injustice in the heroic age. Concubinage, even open concubinage, was permitted to husbands but not to wives.[6] Yet here, too, Homer may have introduced a refinement. He implies that happily married men avoided the practice. During the Trojan campaign Menelaus and Odysseus had no concubines,[7] in contrast with the unhappy Agamemnon and Achilles. But Homer makes it clear that husbands might have other motives for avoiding concubinage. In the first book of the *Odyssey* he mentions the fact that Laertes bought Eurycleia for a large price and honored her like a true wife in his house, but avoided cohabiting with her "because he feared the anger of his wife." The implication is that while concubinage was the usual custom Anticleia was a formidable wife, as the daughter of Autolycus might well have been. Laertes' motive for abstinence was fear. Menelaus' was his lasting infatuation for Helen. Odysseus' was, most likely, affection mixed with prudence. Without his being either afraid of Penelope or infatuated with her, his affection for her merged in his desire to preserve the unity of his home, and his faithfulness was doubly secure.

How, then, can Odysseus' liaisons with Circe and Calypso be reconciled with this fidelity? And how can they be reconciled with the later view of Stoics and Christians that Odysseus' conduct in the *Odyssey* provided a pattern of virtue and wisdom? Why, too, did Penelope, who had herself remained strictly chaste for almost twenty years, refrain from reproaching Odysseus when he told her about Circe and Calypso? Circumstances alter cases: it will be well first to consider the circumstances.

At first sight Calypso and Circe seem to have much in common; both are described as "beautiful-haired, dread, vocal" goddesses; both reside in magically beautiful lands; and both, having received Odysseus into their homes when he is in need of peace and rest, hold him in their sway for a long while. But when Homer has developed the characterization of each and has painted in the details of their environment, a strong contrast emerges, a contrast as between darkness and light, between prototypes of the *femme fatale* of sadistic romance and of the gentle Solveig of Ibsen's *Peer Gynt*.

Circe is the first woman Odysseus meets on his wanderings. He arrives at her country after a series of disasters which have shattered the morale of his few remaining companions. Homer warns his audience by a genealogical clue to expect something sinister in what follows. He describes Circe as a sister of the darkly malevolent Aietes, King of Colchis (and thereby an aunt of the baneful enchantress Medea). But she is also the daughter of the lifegiving Sun. Odysseus himself does not know about this significant ancestry until later. But a note of sinister magic is felt as soon as the companions see her palace, where it lies in the heart of a thick wood, patrolled by wolves and lions. In subsequent descriptions Homer builds up a brilliant contrast between the general atmosphere of luxurious beauty in Circe's palace and the latent horror of her enchantments. She is no Gothic witch-hag scrabbling among cats and bats in a murky hut, but a luminous demonic creature combining two equally dangerous but quite dissimilar personalities. As the sister of Aietes she turns men into swine; as a daughter of the Sun she delights them with every sensuous joy. It was left to later allegorists to assert that these were two ways of saying the same thing: the sensual man is the swinish man. The Cynics, always jealous for the good name of the lower animals, argued that perhaps the pigs were the happier of the two.[8]

The story of how Odysseus, forewarned by Hermes and protected by the plant called moly, overcame Circe and rescued his companions needs no retelling. A few details are significant for the present study. When Circe's potion has failed to work and Odysseus threatens her with his drawn sword, she falls at his feet in amazement and fear. Then, recognizing him as the hero, whose coming had been predicted to her by Hermes, she at once invites him to her couch "so that by loving they may have trust in each other." The abruptness of her invitation—though it may be due partly to the condensed style of these folk-tale episodes in Odysseus' wanderings—might well have surprised even the alert Odysseus if Hermes had not already prophesied it. Odysseus, following Hermes' advice, and his own instincts of prudence, makes Circe swear an oath not to harm him when he is unarmed, and accedes to her request. Later a feast is brought to them. But Odysseus cannot eat for thinking of his companions in the pigsties. Circe assumes that he is thinking of his own safety and reminds him of her oath. This is characteristic of her *égoïsme à deux*. It never occurs to her that anything outside his own personal welfare (which she now identifies with her own) can concern him. Odysseus' reply contains a mild rebuke: "What decent man could bear to feast before freeing and seeing his comrades?" Circe promptly goes and transforms them back into younger and handsomer men than they were before. When they and Odysseus burst into loud lamentations together she ("even she," as Homer puts it) feels an altruistic emotion for the first time and pities them. Then, having realized the deep bond of loyalty that unites Odysseus with his crew, she invites him to bring the others from his ship so that they may all stay and recuperate with her for a while. Madame Wolf has become a Florence Nightingale, it seems.

The result of Circe's new policy of kindness towards Odysseus and his companions was that very soon Odysseus fell completely under her sway. A year passed before any move was made to continue their voyage home. In the end it was the companions who had to approach Odysseus and remind him of his destiny. Their words suggest a mixture of bewilderment and diffidence.[9] Having heard them, Odysseus neither apologizes nor procrastinates. That evening he abjectly beseeches Circe to fulfil her promise to send him on his way home. She makes no effort to detain him against his will. She simply warns him of further perils on his homeward journey.

Two features of this are noteworthy. First there is the complete reversal of Odysseus' mastery of Circe. He who a year ago had brought her as a suppliant to his knees is now humbly supplicating her help. Secondly there is the complete absence of affection in their last words together. Here the contrast with Calypso is most marked. Circe, even when she has adopted a policy of winning by kindness, instead of subduing by witchcraft, shows none of Calypso's warm affectionateness. Though capable of pity and eager for physical love with a hero, she is primarily a dispassionate enchantress intent on having her own way—*la belle dame sans merci*. She is not, indeed, the vampirish monster of nineteenth-century sensationalism; but there is something inhuman and predatory in her. Perhaps once more this is because Homer had not completely assimilated a traditional figure to his more humanistic style, so that the abruptness of her actions is more that of a marionette than of a fully developed character. But, taken in its general context, her conduct has a sinister automaton-like effect, quite unlike Calypso's manner. She never entirely steps out of that world of fairytale which in such an alarming way anticipates the robot-like figures of modern scientific fiction.

In contrast with Circe's nonchalance in parting with Odysseus once his comrades had reawakened his desire to return to Ithaca, Calypso does all she can to keep him for ever. Homer records nothing about the first seven years of Odysseus' life with her, except that when he was shipwrecked on her shore she "received him with loving kindness, and tended him, and said that she would make him immortally youthful," and that afterwards she had always treated him "like a god." After his visit to the Land of Ghosts and his encounters with Scylla, Charybdis, and the Cattle of the Sun, Calypso's gentle kindness and the languorous, relaxing beauty of her island must have come to him like balm from Gilead. But at the very beginning of the *Odyssey* Homer takes care to show that Calypso's attentions did not succeed in killing Odysseus' desire for home. Athene emphasizes this in her first speech to Zeus in Book One:

> But grief and rage alternate wound my breast
> For brave Ulysses, still by fate oppress'd.
> Amidst an isle, around whose rocky shore
> The forests murmur, and the surges roar,
> The blameless hero from his wish'd for home
> A goddess guards in her enchanted dome.
> Atlas her sire. . . .
> By his fair daughter is the chief confined
> Who soothes to dear delight his anxious mind:
> Successless all her soft caresses prove,
> To banish from his breast his country's love;
> To see the smoke from his loved palace rise,
> While the dear isle in distant prospect lies
> With what contentment would he close his eyes!
> (Pope's amplified version)

Similarly when Odysseus first appears personally in the narrative, in Book Five, he is sitting on a headland with his eyes full of tears, gazing across the sea. Every day, we are told, he used to leave Calypso's cave to haunt the rocky promontories, sobbing and groaning in agonies of homesickness, his spirit wasting away with yearning for home. It is clear that Homer wished none of his hearers to be in doubt on this point. He tells how at night Odysseus would indeed sleep beside the nymph, but only—cruel phrase—unwillingly and perforce.[10] Yet Calypso even in her parting scenes with this reluctant consort never expresses any bitterness or anger. The most she allows herself is a touch of scorn at his refusal to accept her offer of immortal youth. Even when she smiles to see how characteristically he distrusts the news of his release, she takes away the sting with an affectionate touch of her hand.

Unlike Circe, Calypso uses all the wisdom and prescience of a minor divinity to study Odysseus' thoughts and inclinations. She fully understands his yearnings for home and his eagerness to escape from his exile with her. Yet she continues to hope until the end that he may change his mind. When Hermes comes at the bidding of Zeus (prompted by Athene) and tells her that she must send Odysseus away, she is angry with what she considers a typical example of Olympian envy and spite. She makes a last effort to persuade him to stay. After a lavish banquet, she warns Odysseus of the trials he must undergo even when he has returned to Ithaca, and suggests that he would be much wiser to accept her offer of immortal life in Ogygia with her. She reminds him that, after all, Penelope is only a mortal woman whose beauty cannot compare with a goddess's. (Behind her words, as Odysseus realizes, stands the spectre, so much dreaded by the Greeks, of feeble, ugly old age.) But she fails to persuade him. He admits that Penelope cannot compete with her in beauty (just as barren Ithaca, Homer implies, could not rival the violet-strewn meadows of Ogygia where "even a god would find wonder and delight"). Yet, no matter what troubles await him, he wants to go home. He says nothing about love or affection, but simply insists that home is best. Calypso knows that she is defeated. After Odysseus has built his boat she dresses herself in a beautifully perfumed robe—Homer deftly suggests a variety of fragrances in Ogygia—sees to his provisions for the voyage, arranges for a "warm and harmless breeze" to waft him away, watches him as he joyfully spreads his sails for home—and turns back, alone, to her cave.

Why did she fail to hold Odysseus? Apart from the technical reason that the plot of the *Odyssey* demanded Odysseus' return to Ithaca, Odysseus' own nature precluded it. Homer always insisted that Odysseus' love of home was his dominant desire, symbolized in the much-borrowed image of "the smoke rising up from his own land."[11] What was the essence of this devotion? A modern romantic novelist might tend to concentrate it in an all-absorbing love for Penelope. To an early classical writer this would seem little different from infatuation and folly in an adult hero. As Homer saw it Penelope was at the

centre of Odysseus' affections partly because of her own personal qualities but partly also because she stood for the whole texture of Odysseus' normal life in Ithaca, the life which he had been unwilling to leave when the call came to join the expedition against Troy. It would be otiose guesswork to try to mark a clear division between Odysseus' love for Penelope and his love for his home and kingdom. In Calypso's Ogygia they were part of one complex feeling in Odysseus' heart—his yearning for a normal, natural, sociable life as husband, father, and king.[12]

Here one sees a radical contrast between Homer's conception of Odysseus and that of many later writers on the Ulysses theme. The movement of the *Odyssey* is essentially inwards, homewards, towards normality. As conceived later by poets like Dante, Tennyson, and Pascoli, Ulysses' urge is centrifugal, outwards towards the exotic or abnormal. As Pascoli sees it, when Odysseus returns to Ithaca he will be irresistibly drawn back to Calypso and to her mystical island.[13] There at last, after many mysterious experiences in the scenes of his Odyssean wanderings, he will find peace in the shadow of her cloud-like hair and be blissfully absorbed into Nirvanic annihilation.

This is, of course, mainly a fantasy of late nineteenth-century aestheticism. But Pascoli's superbly evocative descriptions of Calypso's island bring out a significant feature in Homer's narrative. Homer's account of Ogygia, that flower-strewn, aromatic island, does suggest something of the *dolce far niente,*[14] in implicit contrast with the rugged, harsh Ithaca which Odysseus so deeply loved. Modern attitudes must not be allowed to cause confusion here. The languorous life of the South Sea Islands has attracted many Europeans in the last century—Gauguin, for example, to Tahiti, Stevenson to Samoa. But such a life of idle hedonism would never satisfy an early Greek, eager for action, society, and renown—least of all a hero so much endowed with practical ability as Odysseus. When Aristotle defined happiness as a manly (or "virtuous") activity of the vital powers, he was echoing what Achilles had said to Odysseus in the Land of Ghosts: better to be the basest of farm laborers on earth than, without bodily strength and physical activity, to lord it over all the hosts of the dead. Calypso's mistake was to think that a man like Odysseus could ever be happy among the violets and the vines of Ogygia. Better, as he told her, the severest sufferings of war or sea-voyaging than that perfume-drugged lethargy, that voluptuous sloth, even with a goddess to love and tend him.

If these are true interpretations of Odysseus' relationships with Circe and Calypso, the answers to the questions posed earlier become clear. The reason why Homer, Penelope, and the moralists of the later tradition, did not think ill of Odysseus for these infidelities was primarily because in both cases Odysseus was not acting voluntarily. Both Circe and Calypso were demigoddesses endowed with power to compel their will. Before Odysseus met Circe, Hermes had given him a specific command to grant her request to become her consort. With Calypso there was no direct command from Zeus,[15] but the circumstances were such as to overpower any man of classical antiquity, except perhaps Socrates. Besides, as Penelope would well know in those god-frequented times, to reject the advances of divinities was dangerous indeed. She would hardly have preferred him to be turned into a tree like Daphne or into an ineffectual prophet like Cassandra. Just what else Penelope may have thought in her heart Homer does not suggest. He is satisfied to make it clear that either through affection or through prudence she expressed no annoyance when Odysseus told her his story. The joy of their final reunion was left unclouded. Doubtless Homer intended his hearers to appreciate the contrast with Clytaemnestra's murderous reception of Agamemnon after his infidelities at Troy.[16]

But what of Nausicaa? One might have thought that inclinations to see Odysseus as a sentimental or Byronic amorist would have been checked by consideration of his behavior with her in Phaeacia. But it is not so. In late Victorian times a young poet, afterwards a distinguished Professor of Poetry,[17] went so far as to suggest that the happiest ending for Odysseus' life would be to return to Nausicaa and live happily ever after in Phaeacia; and more recently a generally sympathetic interpreter of the *Odyssey*,[18] while admitting that there is no real love story in Homer's account of the incident, has recorded his sadness at its absence. This demands some explanation.

Odysseus' first encounter with Nausicaa was perhaps the severest test of tact and resourcefulness in his whole career. He has been sleeping on the Phaeacian shore exhausted, foul, and naked, after his long ordeal at sea under Poseidon's wrath. His condition is much as it must have been when he was shipwrecked on Calypso's island—but

Homer to avoid repetition did not describe that scene. There is, however, a psychological difference. Calypso was a mature and kindly goddess. Odysseus has now to deal with an inexperienced young girl. How will she react to the sight of a naked stranger when he appears suddenly beside her? It will need all Odysseus' adroitness to keep this situation in hand.

As soon as the ugly apparition is seen coming from the thicket, Nausicaa's handmaidens scatter in flight. But she herself, strengthened by Athene (just as it was by Athene's prompting that she had gone to this part of the seashore), stands her ground. Odysseus approaches her and speaks. His speech is very carefully phrased, and shows a remarkable delicacy of feeling. Perhaps Odysseus was helped by remembering that if Penelope had borne him a daughter before he had gone to Troy she would be about Nausicaa's age or a little older by now. Or perhaps, he remembered his own sister Ctimene when they were young together. So, at least, his gentle sensibility towards a young unmarried girl's feelings suggests.

He begins by expressing awe and admiration for her Artemis-like beauty (that is, slender, virginal, athletic, in contrast, it is implied, with the more voluptuous charms of Aphrodite). Then he blesses the father, mother, and brothers of such a maiden—how their hearts must be gladdened to see her gracefulness in the festive dances! (Odysseus had guessed that Nausicaa, like most girls of her age, likes dancing.) Happier still, he respectfully adds, the man who is to marry her. (A married girl would hardly have been playing like this with maidens on the seashore.) A deft comparison of her slender stature with a palm-tree at Delos enables him to imply that he himself is a man who goes on religious pilgrimages with a large retinue—no irreligious tramp, whatever his present appearance suggests. And he has suffered many woes (this to touch her tender heart); and more sufferings await him. This said, he appeals directly to her pity. She is the first fellow-creature that he has met and supplicated since his last shipwreck. Will she give him even a wrapping of her laundry to clothe himself in (he falls into a beggar's mock humility for a moment—a part he had played before at Troy and must play painfully soon again in Ithaca), and show him the way to the town? He ends with a wish that must have come from the heart of a man separated for so long from his own wife:

Then may the gods give you all that your heart is desiring,
Husband, and home. And the joy of united hearts may they grant you—
For what in all that Heaven can grant is better or stronger
Than when husband and wife in oneness of heart share their household together?

Nausicaa's first reply is what one would expect from a well-bred, brave, but naturally rather overwhelmed, girl in this unusual situation. It must have sounded prim at first in contrast with the kind of talk Odysseus had been used to for the last eighteen years among warriors, divinities, and monsters. She tells him that he doesn't look like an evil or foolish man. Why then has he suffered so much, if he did not deserve heaven's wrath?—a nice, but somewhat untimely theological question. But she has been well instructed. She knows the answer: Zeus sometimes apportions prosperity to evil men and misfortune to good men. Fortunately for the patience of Odysseus, she puts this very briefly and does not pause to discuss why Zeus is so arbitrary. She is a pious girl, but not inhumanly so. In her next words she promises the persuasive stranger all he has asked.

One need not examine the rest of the scene in detail, for its characterization is mainly devoted to Nausicaa, not to Odysseus. She has been criticized harshly for remarking to her attendants, after Odysseus had been miraculously beautified by Athene, that he looks like the kind of man she would like to marry.[19] But this is entirely in keeping with her naïve and frank nature, and it is addressed only to her intimate friends. There is obviously no deep personal emotion involved. Every day in the cinemas of our time adolescents say or think something like this about the handsomer actors and actresses on the screen. It is no more than a romanticized manner of expressing admiration. Here it is Homer's device for reminding us of Odysseus' personal attractiveness.

When Nausicaa has brought Odysseus safely to the town, she leaves him, and we see her only once again in the story. On the evening of the next day she meets Odysseus on his way to the banquet of the Phaeacians.[20] Both she and Odysseus are looking their best, Homer emphasizes. Odysseus has just been bathed and is wearing a fresh tunic and cloak; Nausicaa is "endowed with beauty from the gods." She speaks first: "Farewell, stranger; and when you are in your native land see that you remember me, for it is to me that you owe the saving of your life." Odysseus replies: "Nausicaa, daughter of magnanimous Alcinous, may Zeus . . . grant that I reach home and see the day of my return! Then surely will I offer thanksgivings to you there as to a god, always, every day, as now: for it was you who gave me life, maiden." That is all. Nausicaa is never mentioned again in Homer. There is no evidence that Odysseus kept his rather extravagant promise all his life. But it expressed his sincere gratitude and respect.

Some have found this brief parting scene disappointingly curt. "Our heart is disappointed and defrauded of its dues." The relationship, we are told, is "like a musical phrase left incomplete." In other words, if Nausicaa is a fairy princess, why does not Odysseus, the typical stranger-hero, become her lover?[21]

The answer, as elsewhere, is partly stylistic, partly ethical. The final purpose of the *Odyssey,* and of Odysseus within it, is the return and restoration of the prince of Ithaca. Nausicaa plays her minor part in advancing that purpose, and is then firmly bowed out both by Homer and Odysseus. Even if the composer of the *Odyssey* had been a woman (as Samuel Butler and an ancient critic believed), she would hardly have made it otherwise. The classical style demands strict subordination of the parts to the whole, of the episodes to the final purpose. And from the point of view of ethics Penelope would have had good reason to view any liaison between her husband and Nausicaa very differently from the Circe and Calypso incidents. There was no supernatural sanction on Nausicaa's side.

Suppose Odysseus and this *princesse lointaine* had become lovers, what would have been the likeliest result? Goethe,[22] with his profound insight into Homer's world, saw that any such relationship between the grizzled veteran and this unsophisticated girl would only bring tragedy to the weaker one. Homer or Goethe could have produced another Dido and Aeneas story here, if they had wished. But would it have pleased admirers of Nausicaa more than the idyll as it is now in the *Odyssey?* The other alternative—to imagine a starry-eyed Odysseus wandering blissfully hand in hand on the Phaeacian shore with his young bride Nausicaa happily ever after[23]—belongs to the world of Peter Pan, not of Homer or Goethe. Homer avoided both a tragic and a novelettish crisis, refusing to let an episode become a major theme. And at the same time he implied that Odysseus was neither a philandering Don Juan gathering rosebuds while he may, nor a home-forsaking Byron.

What of Penelope herself? The conventions of successive romantic eras in European literature, from the troubadours to the neo-Hellenists, have been hard on faithful Penelopes. It would take a whole volume to free her from the accumulated disparagements of centuries. The gravest injustice is to compare her, after nineteen years of anxious waiting, burdened with the cares of a young son and an unruly household, with the carefree Nausicaa, Circe, and Calypso, or with the petted and wayward Helen. A recent Swedish writer has solved this time-problem by portraying her on Odysseus' return as if she had not changed in looks or in mind since her bridal day in Lacedaemon twenty years ago. But Homer presents real men and women, not dream-fantasies. He does not hesitate to reveal the ravages of her long vigil.

For the first ten years, while Odysseus was still with the Achaean chieftains on the Trojan campaign, Penelope had simply to contend with her loneliness and the normal problems of a household whose master is absent. But when, after the sack of Troy, Odysseus failed to return in due time, her difficulties became much more severe. Then she had to cope with the obstreperous attentions of over a hundred lusty suitors insolently frequenting her house and devouring its substance; she had to manage disloyal servants; she had to control a vigorous and rather unsympathetic son in the uncertainties of his approaching manhood. It is hardly surprising, then, that when Odysseus returns in the twentieth year of her ordeal he finds her nerves frayed and her heart almost frozen with despair.[24]

Homer arranges for two major scenes between the long-separated husband and wife. In the first Odysseus is still disguised as a beggar, and Penelope does not recognize him. Yet, as has been recently argued, this scene acquires much greater dramatic and psychological force if it is understood that by the end of it Penelope has reached the point of feeling that this stranger may be, even must be, Odysseus at last.[25] According to this view Odysseus, too, knows that Penelope is by now almost convinced of his identity, but does not try to give her final proof until the suitors have been killed. The situation, then, in their first conversations will be like that in De la Mare's novel,

The Return, where a man comes back to his wife with his face completely changed by black magic (just as Odysseus has been transformed by Athene). During his first interview with his bewildered wife he thinks: "She is pretending; she is trying me; she is feeling her way . . . she knows I *am* I, but hasn't the courage." Odysseus is less detached, less self-conscious, and has more pity for his wife's sufferings than this modern schizophrene. But the two situations are fundamentally similar in their mixture of hope, fear, faith, and doubt.

Some aspects of Odysseus' conduct in the first scene[26] deserve special attention. He is reluctant at first to tell Penelope a flat lie in reply to her inquiry about who he is: on other occasions he is much readier with pseudo-autobiographies. Sometimes he speaks with a brusqueness one would expect more from a husband than from a beggar speaking to a queen. When Penelópe shows deep emotion at his references to her missing lord, Odysseus has to hold his eyes "as unflinching as horn or iron" to avoid weeping with her. Homer implies that it was one of the sternest tests of self-control that Odysseus had ever experienced. In fact he did begin to weep but hid his tears by a trick. But in this scene attention is mainly focused on Penelope, as she so fully deserves, and on the poignancy of her conflicting thoughts and feelings.

When, after the killing of the suitors, Eurycleia goes to tell Penelope that Odysseus is home and has triumphed, Homer's skill in portraying personal feelings reaches its height. He refuses to rush to his climax, the recognition of husband and wife, as a cruder story-teller might have done. Instead, like an expert musician he increases the final effect by an unexpected diminuendo and by some wavering, indecisive modulations before the final diapason chords are struck. In the slowness of Penelope to accept the happy truth one sees the epic style at its best. At this level it rivals the finest achievements of dramatic art—in this tolerance of personal dubieties and uncertainties and hesitations and rebuffs, and in the ability to use them as elements in its full symphonic plan. In works of lesser genius, in the Ulysses tradition as well as outside it, one is often painfully conscious of a conflict between the exigencies of form and those of characterization. Here in *Odyssey* Twenty-three Homer unites form and content in a superb integration of art and life, so that one can say in the same breath "How true" and "How finely handled." Perhaps some of

Homer's original hearers were impatient, like Telemachus in the story, for the final reunion. But modern readers who are prepared to give Homer the freedom of technique that they give to contemporary writers will not complain.

Detailed analysis of the final recognition scene[27] would be out of place here. The texture of Homer's art is too closely woven to permit any effective substitute for itself. The feature most worthy of notice is Penelope's victory. Up to this point Odysseus had been very confident and very patient in accepting his wife's doubts and reservations about his identity. He had rebuked Telemachus for trying to hurry her into accepting him, and had left her alone for a while to make up her mind in her own way. Now he has returned again, cleansed from the gore of battle, finely clothed, and specially beautified by Athene. Certain that he is irresistible now, he addresses Penelope in almost the same chiding terms which Telemachus had used earlier. He is astonished at the unwomanlike hardness of her heart: surely no other wife would behave like this towards a long-lost husband. Penelope's reply shows that she is no more to be intimidated by her husband than by her son. "I am equally surprised at you," she replies, "and I am not the one who has got things out of proportion." Then (after an ambiguous phrase which could imply that she no longer doubts his identity) she deftly springs her trap in an offhand remark about his special bed. Her implication that it can be moved from its place takes Odysseus completely aback—it "pains his heart." Revealing his deeper feelings spontaneously for the first time since his return home, "he indignantly addresses his clever-witted wife." Who has tampered with their unique bed, the finest product of his skill in carpentry? Penelope's purpose is achieved. She has deflated Odysseus' self-confidence, and she can be certain that he is really Odysseus—for when is a man more uniquely himself than in indignation and surprise at some interference with his special possessions?[28] Having triumphed, Penelope crowns her victory with complete surrender. Bursting into tears, she throws her arms about her husband, kisses him, and begs that he will not be angry with her. To Odysseus, as Homer says in a carefully chosen simile, this is like the sight of land to shipwrecked mariners. Though he has further trials to face before the *Odyssey* is completed —"Home is the sailor, home from sea."

In these progressive stages of the final reconciliation of husband and wife Homer had three main problems. The first was to find adequate and convincing expression for the release of so much accumulated emotion. The second was to portray a Penelope worthy of his Odysseus. Feminists may dislike this, but despite the poet's admiration for feminine qualities it can hardly be denied that Odysseus is the pivot of his poem. The third was to give a unique and memorable quality to the final dénouement. Few who can read Greek will deny his success in the first. For the second, even the few illustrations given in this chapter should suffice to display how well matched these two are in quick perception, intelligence, caution, endurance, subtlety, affection, and deep emotion (which is naturally less restrained in Penelope). Homer succeeds in the third partly by superb constructional devices—carefully calculated approaches and withdrawals, diminuendo and crescendo, as already suggested—and partly by introducing an element of paradox, noticed by an ancient commentator.[29] This last quality consists mainly in Penelope's unpredictable changes of mood—pessimistic, optimistic, sceptical, trusting, merry, sad. But the culmination comes at the very end, when to Odysseus' surprise, as well as ours, it is Penelope who plans and executes the final test of Odysseus' identity. Once again Homer has paid a high tribute to woman's intelligence. Already another woman, Eurycleia, had been quicker than Odysseus had anticipated, when she perceived the scar and immediately guessed who he was. But this had been accidental. Penelope's triumph was planned and achieved by her own wit alone.

Another aspect of their final recognition scene has been neglected. Thanks to the poet's skill and Penelope's resourcefulness, Odysseus is virtually compelled in the end to woo her again as he wooed her some twenty years before in Sparta. He compliments her, chides her, puzzles her, entertains her, flatters her, is patient with her, gives her confidence, makes her doubtful; he exhibits his strength, his feats of arms, his courage, his prudence, his resourcefulness, his forbearance, his gentleness, his understanding; he boasts a little, praises himself a good deal, smiles, sets his face like stone, is angry, cajoles, bullies. And, most significantly for Penelope's status, it is when he begins to bully and chide her that she trips him up and outwits him. Yet—and this is her greatest moral triumph—once she has got the effect she wanted by her subterfuge, instead of boasting and making Odysseus admit that she can be cleverer than he, when she likes, she simply yields.

There is something of the profoundest significance in this final self-abandonment. As Eustathius, Bishop of Thessalonica (to whose compilation of ancient commentaries these chapters owe much), remarks, Penelope's problem about the stranger was really insoluble: for if the stranger was (as she feared) a god in the guise of her husband, what was to prevent him in his omniscience from knowing even the Secret of the Bed?[30] This is the kind of difficulty that belief in non-moral polymorphous divinities constantly creates in archaic literature, especially among a witty and logical people like the Greeks. Homer makes Penelope solve it boldly by an act of intuitive faith. Intelligence cannot lead her the whole way. She must make a leap of faith—in this case to reject a hypothesis of divine action. So Penelope is more than just a clever, faithful wife. She personifies that universal affirmation, that spirit of self-abandoning surrender, which is woman's answer to man's negations and resistances to life. Her final submission to Odysseus is not a defeat. It is a paradoxical triumph of self-giving.

Homer says less about Odysseus' other family relationships. Two references in the *Iliad,* as already quoted, agree with many indications in the *Odyssey* in implying that Odysseus was proud of having a son and heir. But when he and Telemachus meet at last, and in their subsequent actions together, their conversations seem distinctly formal, almost hollow, compared with those between Odysseus and Penelope. This is another example of Homer's fidelity to life. Telemachus had been an infant in arms when Odysseus left for Troy: now he is a sensitive idealistic young man, like the young Apollo of Frances Cornford's epigram:

> Magnificently unprepared
> For the long littleness of life.

He and his father have almost nothing in common either in experience or in outlook. Though they share a strong sense of belonging to each other, this is still an entirely *a priori* bond of feeling—a cherished hypothesis without any empirical proof as yet. For nearly twenty years each has thought and wondered about the other. Now, when their hopes and anxieties are to be put to the touchstone of reality, what will the result be—love or hate? Odysseus with his knowledge of life, would be fully aware of the subtle tensions in a relationship like this. Telemachus, whose characteristic epithet in the *Odyssey* means "well endowed with intelligence,"[31] would intuitively apprehend them. That is why Homer keeps their relationship rather formal and rather guarded, though each is always ready to meet the other half-way, until the end of the *Odyssey*. It would have been false to equate so unsubstantial an intimacy as this with the profound empirical understanding of husband and wife. Yet this father-son relationship is one of the deeper elements in the Ulysses myth. Writers in the later tradition make much of it.[32]

Odysseus' last reunion in the *Odyssey* is with his father Laertes.[33] Homer enlists our sympathy for the old man's plight by first revealing him as he works with his hoe among the briars of an outlying farm. His tunic is patched and dirty. As protection against the rending thorns he wears leggings and mittens on the limbs that once had shone in heroic armor. His helmet is now a goatskin cap. He is alone, bending low over his work. Odysseus sees all this as he stands among the trees which Laertes had given him as a boy. Naturally he weeps at the sight. But was it simply caution that prompted him to postpone revealing his true identity at once, and to "test" his father with another fictitious tale? Homer in an introductory phrase[34] suggests something more, something that we can hardly admire in Odysseus here—a touch of sly mockery. And, indeed, Odysseus' first words do seem to show a trace of this:

> Old man, you have everything so tidy here that I can see there is little about gardening that you do not know. . . . On the other hand, I cannot help remarking, I hope without offence, that you don't look after yourself very well; in fact, what with your squalor and your wretched clothes, old age has hit you very hard. Yet it can't be on account of any laziness that your master neglects you, nor is there anything in your build and size to suggest the slave. (Rieu's translation)

Odysseus goes on to spin out a rigmarole about this and that until "a dark cloud of woe" covers Laertes. In an agony of grief the old man fills his hands with dust from the ground and pours it in utter despair down over his grey head. Then a sudden spasm of feeling seizes

Odysseus. To express its unusual force Homer uses a unique phrase—"a pungent spirit thrust its way down his nostrils." He leaps forward, embraces his father, kisses him, and in broken phrases reveals himself. Laertes demands proof of his identity, as well he might after Odysseus' earlier conduct. He is easily convinced. Embracing Odysseus in turn, he faints, overpowered by emotion, in his arms.

The scene is full of deep psychological undercurrents: but, as usual, Homer declines to explain them. It can only be a guess, to be accepted or rebutted by each reader for himself as he reconsiders the episode, that the poet is suggesting a latent father-son antagonism here. (One does not need to discourse on Oedipus complexes to admit the frequency of such a relationship, and there is nothing Oedipus-like in Odysseus.) Though the tradition never refers to any open conflict, Homer does imply, without explaining it, that Laertes had resigned from his kingship before Odysseus went to Troy. Since after twenty years Laertes was still vigorous enough to hoe a plantation (and in the final scene of the *Odyssey,* to don armor and, with Athene's help, to kill an enemy) this early abdication was curious. If he and his son, then perhaps about twenty-five, had reached a state of strong, but not ungovernable, antagonism, the action would be one of wise and generous policy on Laertes' part.

In contrast Odysseus' interview with the spirit of his mother Anticleia in the Land of Ghosts implies a deep and fully sympathetic relationship. Despite its brevity and its comparative unimportance in the development of the plot, the scene is one of the most memorable in the Homeric poems, and it was constantly imitated by later writers. Odysseus' primary purpose in visiting Ghost-land on Circe's instructions was to consult the spirit of the prophet Teiresias about his return to Ithaca. To his surprise the ghost of Elpenor, the companion accidentally killed in Circe's palace, meets him first, and, after that, Anticleia's. At the sight of his mother's wraith Odysseus bursts into tears. He had not known that she was dead. Yet he does not allow her to come and drink the blood, despite his grief and wonder, until he has first interviewed Teiresias.

This is a shrewd touch of characterization. Homer makes it clear that Odysseus and his mother were most affectionately attached to each other. Yet here Odysseus purposefully—even callously, some may think—postpones all speech with her until his main purpose is achieved. He knows that the safety of both his comrades and himself depends on what Teiresias predicts. The common weal must take precedence over private affections: prudence must prevail over emotion. It is not an exclusively Ulyssean trait. For the same reason Agamemnon consented to the sacrifice of Iphigeneia, Brutus to the execution of his son. On the other hand Homer suggests nothing of the heartlessness of a Nero in Odysseus' action. Odysseus is never presented as an unfeeling or inconsiderate son, father, or husband. But at times he firmly chooses to set the *bonum publicum* above all personal ties. One sees a germ here, but only a germ, of his ruthlessness in the later tradition.

After Teiresias has given his prophecy and retired, Anticleia returns and is allowed to drink the blood. Her first inquiries are for her son. She says nothing of her own fate. Odysseus asks her what caused her death—was it a long or a brief illness?—and what about his father and son?—and what has his wife been thinking?—is she still faithfully looking after Telemachus and the royal possessions or has some noble Achaean married her? His mother with feminine understanding answers his last, but most important, question first[35]: he may rest assured, his wife is still faithful to him "with enduring spirit, though the days and nights ever waste sorrowfully away for her in tears and grief." His son is well and popular. But old Laertes is lonely, neglected, and unhappy on his country estate. (Here, too, Homer dwells on the misery of Laertes' condition.) Finally she tells the cause of her own death. It was not illness that laid her low, but yearning for him, her only son, for his thoughtfulness and for his kindly ways. Odysseus is too much moved to reply at once. He can only stretch out his arms to embrace her. But she is a ghost, and can no more be held than a shadow or a dream. Perplexed and distraught, he asks why she glides from his arms. She, always sorrier for him than for herself—"Alas, my child, unhappiest of mortals," she begins—tells him about the sad, disembodied state of the dead; says good-bye, and, thoughtful for others to the end, devotes her last words to his wife.

Though the scene is full of deep emotion, to deduce (in the manner of modern psychoanalysis) any abnormal relationship between Odysseus and his mother would be rash. The ghost of any other normally affectionate mother would hardly speak differently to her only son, unless he were unusually unlovable. Here Homer presents a typical scene in life—the devoted mother and the busy, rather self-centred, but not entirely inconsiderate or unaffectionate, son—endowing it with a pathos and nobility which the European literary tradition has never forgotten. But the contrast with the much less loving scene between Odysseus and his father may hint that a daughter of Autolycus would be better equipped to understand Odysseus' Autolycan characteristics than a man of more conventional origins like Laertes.

These relationships, with wife, child, parents, and goddesses (including Athene) were the most significant in Odysseus' life. Others Homer mentions more briefly. The noble swineherd Eumaeus obviously admired him with a genuine affection. It must have done much to restore Odysseus' confidence, after his return to Ithaca disguised as a beggar, to hear the warm tributes of that most gentlemanly of pig-keepers.[36] The same kind of loyal affection was more to be expected from Odysseus' old nurse Eurycleia, and Homer does not leave any doubt that Odysseus received it. Some of Odysseus' subjects in Ithaca, too, speak warmly of his paternal benevolence and mildness. It is clear that, whatever his conduct was like at Troy, in his home and homeland he showed nothing of the machine-like disregard of personal feelings which the later tradition found in him.

A few passing incidents deserve some notice. The affability of Alcinous towards Odysseus as his unknown guest cannot be taken as significant. That genial old king seems to have been of the kind to welcome, like Nestor, any new victim for his garrulity. But he seems to have loved his daughter Nausicaa, so that his offer of her hand in marriage to Odysseus was a high tribute to Odysseus' personality—for Alcinous did not yet know the stranger's identity. Queen Arete is quite different. At first she maintains a strong reserve towards Odysseus, conceding nothing beyond her formal protection until over a day after his arrival. She lets Alcinous do all the talking, and is satisfied only to shoot a shrewd question at Odysseus, asking him where he got the clothes he was wearing.[37] (She had, of course, recognized them as some of those which Nausicaa had taken to wash.) After that she says nothing at all until late in the evening of the following day.

It does not seem to have been emphasized before that this is another example of Homer's consummate skill in blending formal construction with characterization. The situation is this: Odysseus has been describing his adventures in the Land of Shades. Is it too much, or too ungenerous, to suppose that while he told about his encounter with his mother's ghost, he was not unaware of the effect it might have on the listening Queen of the Phaeacians? Some (men more than women, perhaps) may be inclined to think this hypocritical and insincere. But the complexities of an artist's mind—and here, under Homer's hand, Odysseus is telling his story with superb rhetorical artistry—are not easily sorted into the simpler ethical categories. When an artist acts a part or heightens the emotion of a past incident he is not necessarily insincere or untrue to himself. Or, to put it specifically, if Odysseus deliberately emphasized or even amplified the emotional aspects of his interview with his mother, in order to present it as effectively as possible to Arete, we may condemn him as an untrustworthy witness, but not as an incompetent story-teller, or entertainer, or after-dinner speaker.

This opens up a psychological complication. It must not be allowed to lead too far from the subject in hand, but it cannot be passed over entirely. In Books Nine to Twelve of the *Odyssey* Homer ostensibly delegates his task as a story-teller to Odysseus. Now comes the problem: does Homer intend us to understand that Odysseus' narrative is factually as precise as it would have been were Homer himself narrating it, or does he intend us to take it as a Ulyssean (and sometimes even Autolycan) version of what "really" took place? To cut the knot it will be assumed that at least occasionally Homer allows Odysseus to adapt his narrative to suit his Phaeacian audience. (And it may be observed that here Odysseus, at the earliest stage of his literary career, speaks for Homer and takes his place as a court entertainer. A later chapter will illustrate how this relationship beween the poet and his creation was made a pretext for maligning them both.)

If Odysseus' purpose in describing the scene with Anticleia was to win Arete's sympathy for a motherless wanderer, he did not let his appeal to the feminine element in his audience end at that. As his next experience he describes the celebrated pageant of beautiful heroines. This has been impugned as a Boeotian accretion to the original story. But its consequences can hardly be dismissed as irrelevant to the general situation in Phaeacia. Immediately Odysseus has finished his description of the famous women, he breaks off his narrative, suggests it is time for sleep, expresses his eagerness to begin his voyage to Ithaca, and then stops. It can hardly be purely accidental that Arete is the first to break the charmed silence in the shadowy hall, and that now for the first time she expresses approval of him. Could this sudden decision have been entirely independent of Odysseus' story about his mother and his descriptions of the other women? Only if the poet of this episode was indeed such a bungler as some critics would have him. It seems more reasonable to accept the sequence as an intentional piece of motivation. In any case, whether by luck or skill, Odysseus is the gainer. He can reckon Arete now among his friends. His last recorded words in Phaeacia are addressed to her.

Another significant interview with a woman is mentioned but not described in the *Odyssey*. In Book Four, Helen tells Telemachus how, when Odysseus ventured into Troy as a spy in a beggar's disguise, she alone detected him. She had questioned him, and he had tried to evade her inquiries with cunning. Then she insisted on giving him a bath, which, naturally, spoilt his disguise. She assured him with a strong oath that she would not reveal his identity until he had safely returned to the Greek ships. Convinced of her good faith, Odysseus told her all that she had been craving to know about "the mind of the Achaeans."

Homer merely sketches this scene in a few lines before continuing his main narrative. It is surprising that later writers did not make more of it. If one remembers that Helen was no hollow mask of feminine beauty, but, as Homer implies in this part of the *Odyssey,* a person of subtle intelligence and perceptiveness, an interview in such unusual circumstances between her and the cleverest of the Greeks stimulates the imagination. There is one unfortunate uncertainty in the Homeric context. Does Homer intend his readers to know that Odysseus had been among the suitors of Helen? If one could assume that this legend was already current in Homer's time and accepted (even though not mentioned) by him, the dramatic quality of this meeting would be greatly enhanced.

One general feature emerges from this study of Odysseus' more intimate personal relationships. He seems to have met none of the suspicion and distrust of his male associates among the women who knew him well. Their greater sympathy and tolerance cannot be explained entirely as a consequence of tenderer natures. Circe and Helen were hardly of that kind, or Athene either. It seems, rather, that Homer intended to imply a closer temperamental affinity between Odysseus and the women of the Heroic Age than between him and the more conventional warrior-heroes who felt uneasy and distrustful in his company. Not that there was any specifically feminine element in Odysseus' nature, but rather that he and Homer's women shared qualities not to be found in his male associates. Athene stated them clearly in the scene described in the last chapter. It was because of Odysseus' civilized gentleness, his intuitive intelligence, and his firm self-possession, that she would not "leave him in misfortune." In an age of violence and infidelity these were qualities that every sensible woman would value.

There was another reason. That Ulyssean versatility, which clashed with the more rigid standards of the typical hero, that power of changing one's manner to suit the occasion, would not antagonize or repel intelligent women; for what was it but a form of that feminine *varium et mutabile* quality which has so long irritated and baffled the more conventional of men?

III

The Odyssey and the Western World

GEORGE DEF. LORD

MR. ELIOT's recent article, "Vergil and the Western World" (*Sewanee Review,* Winter, 1953), has redefined for us the Christian-like qualities of the *Aeneid* and its hero. Virgil is seen as a sort of prophet, perhaps unconsciously inspired by Judaic thought, who anticipated some of the values of the Christian world. The *pietas* of Aeneas requires his acceptance, at the cost of his personal feelings, of a mission on which a future civilization depends, and this acceptance requires the subjection of his own will with all humility to the will of the gods. Aeneas' mission is everything, its fulfillment ordained by destiny, and yet destiny does not relieve him of moral responsibility for its fulfillment. Thus Virgil fills "a significant, a unique place, at the end of the pre-Christian and at the beginning of the Christian world."

Mr. Eliot's description of the unique place which Virgil fills in the evolution of Western culture seems to me invaluable for a proper understanding of the *Aeneid.* But the occasional comments that he makes on the *Odyssey* in the course of defining the spiritual qualities of the *Aeneid* give, I think, a wrong impression of Homer's poem. His discussion of Aeneas as "an analogue and foreshadow of Christian humility" is brilliant in itself, but when he tries to show the superiority of Virgil's hero to Homer's heroes he misconceives or underestimates the character of Odysseus and the part it must have played, consciously or not, in the Roman poet's conception of Aeneas. The *Odyssey* presents through the experiences of its hero the birth of personal and social ideals which are remarkably close to those of the

Reprinted by permission from *The Sewanee Review,* LXII (Summer, 1954), 406–427.

Christian tradition and repudiates the old code of the heroic warriors at Troy as resolutely as does the *Aeneid.* In the *Odyssey* we can witness the origin and evolution of values which made the Roman ideal possible. Aeneas could not have been without Odysseus, and the drama of Odysseus lies in his struggle out of chaos toward an order which we can still respect. The conflict between Aeneas and Turnus in the final books of the *Aeneid* epitomizes the victory of the new hero, the builder of a civilization, over the old—one might say obsolete—warrior hero with his narrow tribal loyalties, his jealous personal honor, and his fierce passions, who is, whatever his motives, the foe of reason, order and civilization. Virgil, in Mr. W. F. Jackson Knight's words, "made the contrast between right reason and the dark instinct, as of Turnus devil-possessed, secure, and shewed the pitilessness, and the frightful havoc, of mass impulse, knowing it strangely well." (*Roman Vergil,* p. 135) Like Achilles, possessed with *ate,* Turnus fights for glory, while Aeneas fights for a future. Aeneas can only assume the burden of his great mission when he has renounced personal glory and desperate courage, which are the chief virtues of the old warriors of the *Iliad.* His victory over Turnus at the end of the poem is only possible because of his victory over the Turnus in himself at the beginning of the poem.

The *Odyssey* mediates between these two concepts of the hero—the old and the new. Odysseus grows in the course of his experiences from the shrewd "sacker of cities" to the wise restorer of Ithaca. His success at the end of the poem is not accidental, but founded just as surely as Aeneas' on the subjection of his angry or amorous passions to reason, on his recognition and acceptance of his divine mission, and on harmonizing his own will with the divine will. The gods of the *Iliad* may be, as Mr. Eliot claims, "as irresponsible, as much a prey to their passions, as devoid of public spirit and the sense of fair play, as the heroes," but the gods of the *Odyssey* are just and responsible, and the ideal of the poem is "a more civilized world of dignity, reason and order" like that of the *Aeneid.* Odysseus, admittedly, has a less impressive and consequential mission than Aeneas'. He is not destined to found a world which history shows is our own. But cannot rocky Ithaca be a type of that world? And cannot Odysseus be thought of as having demonstrated in the restoration of his little country virtues which anticipate Aeneas' as a founding father?

The distinction which Mr. Eliot draws between Aeneas and Odysseus in the following passage in my opinion badly misrepresents the meaning of the *Odyssey*. If Odysseus is the irresponsible and lucky hero he describes, the *Odyssey* is of little interest to us except as an adventure story:

> Aeneas is the antithesis, in important respects, of either Achilles or Odysseus. In so far as he is heroic, he is heroic as the original Displaced Person, the fugitive from a ruined city and an obliterated society, of which the few other survivors except his own band languish as slaves of the Greeks. He was not to have, like Ulysses, marvellous and exciting adventures with such occasional erotic episodes as left no canker on the conscience of the wayfarer. He was not to return at last to the remembered hearth-fire, to find an exemplary wife awaiting him, to be reunited to his son, his dog and his servants.

Since Mr. Eliot is only incidentally concerned with the *Odyssey,* and since his comment on Aeneas is so perceptive, the whole matter could well be ignored except for the fact that this misreading of the *Odyssey* is widely held and, I am convinced, blocks the way to one's full understanding and enjoyment of the poem.

Three or four years ago, in the course of studying Chapman's translation of the *Odyssey,* I found a remarkable and apparently little-known book which helped me to understand Chapman's approach while it illuminated the central themes of Homer's poem more fully and convincingly than anything else on the subject I have encountered. Denton J. Snider's *Homer's Odyssey: a Commentary,* published in 1895, is a brilliant demonstration of the spiritual evolution of Odysseus, the moral character of his universe, and the pre-eminence of freedom and moral responsibility throughout the poem:

> The theme . . . deals with the wise man, who, through his intelligence, was able to take Troy, but who has now another and greater problem—the return out of the grand estrangement caused by the Trojan expedition. Spiritual restoration is the key-note of the *Odyssey,* as it is that of all the great Books of Literature. (pp. 7–8)

Much of what I have to say about the *Odyssey* in the following pages is built upon or developed out of Snider's insights, and I hope that this discussion will send readers on to a unique work of Homeric criticism.

The history of criticism of the *Odyssey* from Hellenic times to the present reveals two principal and unreconciled positions. The allegorical interpreters such as Heraclitus,[1] Natalis Comes and Roger Ascham were impelled to defend the poem on ethical grounds by representing Odysseus as a *persona* of reason, virtue, and endurance triumphing over enticements to lust, luxury, and greed. The allegorists concentrated on those adventures most susceptible of their sort of interpretation—especially the hero's encounter with Circe or with the Sirens. The fabulous experiences which Odysseus recounts in Books Nine to Twelve were treated as if they were the whole poem, and those episodes in which the hero was least successful in dealing with temptations or obstacles to his return were either neglected or forced quite arbitarily to reflect the preconceptions of the interpreters. In most of the allegorical accounts one finds a monotonous determination to demonstrate Odysseus' moral perfection on every occasion. Comes' popular compendium of mythology is typical of them all:

> Who then is Ulysses, if not Wisdom, which intrepidly passes through every danger unconquered? And who are Ulysses' companions but the passions of our hearts?

The allegorists' interest is centered on the *Odyssey* as a moral lesson, and the poem is ignored. They tended to find a simple identification of characters and objects with moral abstractions like wisdom, temperance, lust, and passion. The other school, which has prevailed in the last two hundred years, is "realistic" in its approach and refuses to see any ethical significance at all in Odysseus' career. The realists insist on the primitive nature of Homer's characters. Thomas Blackwell was among the first to propose the historical *apologia,* still current, that although Odysseus was a pirate, piracy was considered respectable in those benighted days: "living by Plunder gave a reputation for Spirit and Bravery." This view supposes that whatever the hero does is endorsed by the poet, just as the allegorical view does. Mr. Eliot's own strictures belong to this tradition, and he would, I suppose, approve of the position taken by Mr. C. S. Lewis:

> There is no pretence, indeed no possibility of pretending, that the world, or even Greece, would have been much altered if

> Odysseus had never got home at all. The poem is an adventure story. As far as greatness of subject goes, it is much closer to *Tom Jones* or *Ivanhoe* than to the *Aeneid* or the *Gierusalemme Liberata.* (*A Preface to Paradise Lost,* p. 26)

In the adventure story what happens to the hero is accidental, and the action is largely external. The interest lies in a series of hair-breadth escapes brought about by the hero's cleverness, stamina, and good luck. The *Odyssey* unquestionably provides this sort of interest, but that is not all.

The conception of the *Odyssey* as an adventure story is, I am convinced, as great an obstacle to understanding it as to see it simply as moral allegory. The first view removes it from serious consideration as one of the world's greatest poems; the second ignores its status as a poem altogether. A third view is required that will recognize the *Odyssey's* great spiritual significance at the same time that it recognizes Odysseus as a complex and typically human character. Odysseus' vicissitudes are intimately related to his varying attitudes toward himself, his fellow man, and his gods. Odysseus' "mission" is the greatest known to man—to discover himself and his world and to act effectively in accordance with these discoveries. Such a view as this sees the goal of his return as more than a geographical one and recognizes both the established moral order of the *Odyssey's* universe and the hero's gradual discovery of that order through suffering and error. If the *Odyssey* were as Heraclitus or Comes or Lewis or Eliot represented it, the poem would not have the enduring hold on men's spirits that it has. A morally perfect hero excites no more sympathy than one whose adventures are amoral and therefore accidental and meaningless.

Primary Epic, in Mr. Lewis's terms, is distinguished from Secondary Epic by the absence of "the large national or cosmic subject of super-personal interest." "That kind of greatness," he continues, "arises only when some event can be held to effect a profound and more or less permanent change in the history of the world, as the founding of Rome did, or still more, the fall of man" (*A Preface to Paradise Lost,* p. 28). This distinction as to kinds is undoubtedly a valid one. But the historical consequence of the subject is relatively unimportant if the theme of the epic is typical and universal. Rocky Ithaca may be the type of Rome and Odysseus the prototype of Aeneas. The *Odyssey* has a great design, depite Mr. Lewis, and it cannot be described by "the mere endless up and down, the constant aimless alternations of glory and misery, which make up the terrible phenomenon called a Heroic Age," any more than it can by Mr. Eliot's conception of it as an alternation of marvellous and erotic adventures that leave the hero essentially unchanged.

The chief obstacle to understanding this revolutionary and evolutionary character of the *Odyssey* is the spareness of direct comment or abstract moral statement in the poem. Aeneas' destiny is stated in the invocation, and his moral struggles are unmistakably presented in the encounter with Dido and the intervention of the gods, in his foolhardy last-ditch stand at Troy and the admonitory or prophetic visions of Hector and Iulus, and in the similes which compare him and his companions in their rage to ravening wolves and serpents. (See 2.370 ff.) The *Odyssey* never explicitly associates the hero's return with his moral and spiritual stature in the way that the *Aeneid* identifies the founding of Rome with Aeneas' *pietas*. Homer, furthermore, externalizes psychological and emotional developments in action. Odysseus is not introspective or reflective in the way that Aeneas is.

The best way I know to illustrate the ideas I have been discussing is to focus on one of the great turning-points in Odysseus' career—his experiences from the time of leaving Calypso in Book Five to the beginning of his narrative to the Phaeacians in Book Nine. This passage introduces the hero after our curiosity about him has been wrought to the highest pitch in the four books of the Telemachia, and it marks his escape from the fabulous world in which he has wandered for ten years since leaving Troy into what we may call the real world. This crisis in Odysseus' life is announced by a council of the gods in which Zeus gives orders that the hero is to be released from the island of Calypso and permitted to sail for home. The divine decision has its counterpart in Odysseus' own choice. Calypso offers him immortal life with her, and he rejects the offer in favor of mortal life with Penelope:

> Great goddess, do not be angry with me for this. I know myself that wise Penelope cannot compare with you in beauty or figure, for she is mortal, you immortal and unaging. Nonetheless, day after day, I long to reach home and see the day of my return. And if some god strikes me on the wine-dark sea, I will

take it, for I have a heart inured to affliction. In days gone by I have suffered and toiled greatly in the sea and in war: let this come too. (5.215–224)

The divine machinery which sets Odysseus free through the agency of Hermes, as has often been noted, can stand for, or, perhaps more accurately, is accompanied by, the hero's effective resolution to accept his human lot and leave Calypso's paradise. For many years he has longed to depart, yet the intervention of the gods at this moment is not simply a heavenly rescue party, a Euripidean *deus ex machina.* The elementary resources needed to build and equip the raft have been available on Calypso's island all the seven years Odysseus has been there. What he lacked for a time was the courage to commit himself once more on the deeps to the strenuous dangers attendant upon such a journey, a journey which, Zeus specifies, must be made "with guidance neither of mortal men nor of gods."

The voyage to Phaeacia turns out to be the hardest of all. Odysseus' last encounter with the wrath of Poseidon literally beats him to his knees and drives him once and for all out of the attitude of cocky self-sufficiency which characterized him earlier. The epithet *polutropos* —shifty and resourceful—does not carry unqualified approval, especially when it applies to Odysseus' rugged individualism. The extremities Odysseus suffers after his raft is wrecked compel him to turn to the gods for help. The stages by which he is forced to this final resort dramatize the hero's characteristic reluctance to depend on anyone but himself. When the sea nymph Ino Leucothea out of pity offers him a miraculous veil, he suspects that "one of the immortals is once again weaving a snare for me in bidding me to leave my raft," and determines to cling to the wreckage as long as he can. He still thinks of the gods' hostility as purely arbitrary. A tremendous wave finally forces him to use the veil. But when, after two days and nights in the sea, he comes in sight of the Phaeacian shore, there is nothing but fatal reefs and cliffs beaten by a violent surf. When he tries to cling to rocks he is torn away by the waves and nearly drowned. At last he finds a river-mouth with a shelving beach and makes a spontaneous prayer to the river-god in the name of wanderers and suppliants, who are all sacred to Zeus. At this the river's current is calmed, Odysseus wades ashore, sinks down among the reeds and kisses the earth.

From this moment Odysseus encounters only human foes and human temptations. There are no more one-eyed giants or monstrous sea-goddesses or sorceresses who can turn men into pigs. Nor are there any further conflicts with nature—storms, shipwrecks, whirlpools, or threatening starvation. When he falls asleep in the olive-grove by the Phaeacian shore, the wrath of Poseidon is done with Odysseus, and he awakes into a world of purely human values. The change is marked by a striking simile at the very end of Book Five, when Odysseus sees the grove and feels an impulse of joy and relief:

> he lay down in the midst and heaped over him the fallen leaves. And as a man hides a brand beneath the dark embers in an outlying farm, a man who has no neighbors, and so saves the seed of fire that he may not have to kindle it at some other source, so Odysseus covered himself with leaves. And Athene shed sleep on his eyes that it might cover his lids and quickly free him from toilsome weariness. (5.487–493)

The simile represents the hero's loneliness, exhaustion, and sense of relief as well as his striking capacity for self-preservation in any fatigue or danger. It suggests further than this that here is the essential Odysseus, the very spark of his spirit which no hardships have been able to quench. The realistic detail of the anxious farmer on his lonely farm emphasizes at this stage of the hero's experience the emergence of realistic human adventures.

The phase of supernatural dangers and of the hostility of physical nature which comes between the departure of Odysseus from Troy and his arrival in Phaeacia divides two vastly different human worlds: that of the Trojan war dominated by the heroic code of men and that of family and community life whose values are centered in several extraordinary women—Arete, Nausicaa, Penelope. The great importance of these women in the *Odyssey* has often been discussed. I need not refer the reader to Samuel Butler's facetious thesis that the *Odyssey* must have been written by a woman or to Bentley's remark that the *Iliad* was written for men and the *Odyssey* for women. It can be shown, I think, that the domestic and social values embodied in or emanating from these women act as a critique of the code of the male warrior just as much as the actions of Turnus or Nisus or Euryalus or of Aeneas on the night that Troy fell reveal Virgil's view of the inadequacy of the heroic code. The behavior of warriors is subjected to a searching and critical scrutiny in the *Odyssey,* although not by much direct comment. Its weaknesses are dramatized in Homer's characteristically subtle fashion. It is extremely significant, I think, that Odysseus enters the world of natural and supernatural disasters after committing an act of violence that becomes, because of the formulaic manner in which it is related, the typical crime of the *Odyssey.* In all his pseudo-autobiographies in the last books of the poem, Odysseus describes his troubles as having originated with a piratical raid against unwary townsmen in which the men were slain, the women and children taken as slaves, and a quantity of plunder carried off. In each case the leader is unable to control his men, who become drunken and careless, and an unexpected counterattack takes its toll of the invaders.

Odysseus' unprovoked attack on the town of Ismarus following his departure from ruined Troy is typical of the acts which cast him out of the world of men, if we except his followers, for ten years. This aggression, which, I am told, Grotius cites as the earliest recorded violation of international justice, is not mitigated in Homer by any mention of the Cicones' alliance with the Trojans. Odysseus relates it in laconic fashion at the beginning of Book Nine:

> From Ilios the wind bore me to the Cicones, to Ismarus. I sacked the city and slew the men, and from the city we took their wives and a store of treasure and divided them among us, so that as far as lay in me no man might go defrauded of an equal share. Then I gave orders that we should flee with all speed, but my men, in their folly, did not listen. (9.39–44)

Odysseus loses six men from each ship to the counter-attacking Cicones and is then driven into a world of fantastic terrors, which he describes for four books, by a twelve days' storm. He raises land at the Lotus-eaters, but it is ten years before he sees a human being again, except for his own companions. In his twelve fabulous adventures with monsters, nymphs, demigods, sorceresses, and ghosts he sometimes encounters, as Snider argues, the monstrous personifications of inhuman facets of his own nature, like Polyphemus and the Laestrygonians. In one way or another all these encounters jeopardize his human individuality, or at least that of his followers. His men who eat the lotus lose all memory of home, as he himself does when he hears the Sirens' song:

> Whosoever in ignorance draws near them and hears the Sirens' voices never returns to have his wife and little children stand at his side rejoicing; but the Sirens beguile him with their clear-toned song as they sit in a meadow, with all about them a great heap of bones of mouldering men, and round the bones the skin shrivelling. (12.41–46)

Circe transforms men into pigs who yet retain the same minds they had before. (Is this satirical?) Calypso promises to make him immortal and ageless if he will only live with her forever. But after seven years the delights of this naturalistic paradise have palled to the extent that he is willing to endure any hardship in order to reach home and Penelope. Odysseus' recognition at this point that his innermost identity is inseparably bound up with his home and wife is the key to his escape from the fantastic world, just as his unprovoked attack on society, as represented by Ismarus, opened the door to his entrance into it.

The subject of the *Odyssey* is the return of Odysseus to his home and his reunion with his family. Such a subject, as Chapman remarks in his preface, may seem "jejune and fruitless enough." If, however, the hero can return home and rejoin his family only in the course of discovering his proper relation to the gods and to his fellow men, no greater subject could be imagined, for the familiar and common situations in which these discoveries are made are an earnest that the pursuit of *these* heroic ideals is the right and duty of all men and not the privilege of any particular caste.

Mr. L. A. Post, in his recent book *From Homer to Menander,* makes this point in general terms when he speaks of "new resources or a new attitude in himself" which Odysseus must find "before he can win happiness." But I cannot agree with Mr. Post when he says that after many years with Calypso on her island Odysseus "has nothing new to learn. He must merely display his qualities of craft and courage and restraint." It is true that Odysseus behaves with much more self-control in the second half of the poem. The ordeals he undergoes as a beggar appealing to the hospitality of his wife's suitors—the blows and insults he must suffer without answering their violence—require a self-mastery that he has not shown before. Epictetus and Plutarch found in Odysseus aspects of the Stoic. But Homer's interest in his hero extends far beyond the Stoical qualities of endurance and restraint to pursue the dynamic origins of these and other moral virtues in the human spirit.

The chief importance of the Phaeacian experience lies in its dramatizing a new attitude in Odysseus. His emergence from the supernatural world of Lotus-eaters, Cyclopes, Circe, and Calypso has involved, as I have shown, a recognition of the conditions of being human: mortality, limited power and wisdom, and the need for divine assistance. Odysseus' ready acceptance by Alcinous, Arete, and Nausicaa depends on his acceptance of their own social, religious, and political ideal. Phaeacia has all the earmarks of an ideal civilization with just enough defects to make the whole picture plausible. The Phaeacians are conspicuously peace-loving. They do not use warfare and migrated long ago from a land beset by the godless Cyclopes to this remote place. The gods, they say, are in the habit of visiting them without disguise. They are charitable to strangers. They excel in the arts of peace—in shipbuilding, sailing, spinning and weaving, and so forth. The queen Arete is the real ruler of the kingdom and settles the disputes of her subjects to the invariable satisfaction of both parties. Odysseus kneels to her for permission to sail for Ithaca and by this action pays tribute to the domestic ideals which Arete stands for. Arete is, perhaps, almost impossibly wise and competent, but Nausicaa stands in the foreground as an extraordinarily real young girl. As Mr. Post says, "It is here that the climax of temptation comes for Odysseus. It is characteristic of Homer to make his good woman more tempting than any bad woman could be."

For Odysseus Nausicaa serves as an enchanting vision of the new ideal, just as fading Helen, with her ornamental distaff and her anodynes, provided Telemachus with a *fin de siècle* vision of the heroic past. Nausicaa appeals to Odysseus by virtue of qualities which make his surrender to her impossible: by her hospitality and charity and courage and deep loyalty to the civilized institutions to which he is now dedicated. In her consuming interest in marriage and in family and household affairs he may well see an image of his own wife. Thus he treats her with unwonted tact and restraint. His manner is a judicious mixture of the gallant and the paternal. With the immortal Circe and Calypso Odysseus had no age, but with Nausicaa he is a mature man. Much of the humor in their encounter stems from this discrepancy of ages which attracts them to each other and yet helps to keep them apart. His famous words on their first meeting, when he emerges so delightfully from the underbrush naked and holding an olive-branch modestly before him, set the tone of the whole episode:

> Show me the city and give me some rag to throw about me. . . . For thyself, may the gods grant thee all thy heart desires —a husband and a home and oneness of heart—great gifts. For nothing is finer than when husband and wife live in one house in one accord, a great grief to their foes and a joy to their friends. But they themselves know this best. (6.178–185)

This note is struck again in that exquisite farewell interlude in which Odysseus gently deflects Nausicaa's growing love for him by pretending not to understand her Desdemona-like hints:

> Now when the maids had bathed him and rubbed him with oil and had cast a fine cloak and tunic about him, he came from the bath and went to join the men at their wine. Nausicaa, gifted with beauty by the gods, stood by the doorpost of the hall and watched Odysseus with wonder and spoke to him with winged words:
>
> "Farewell, stranger, and hereafter even in thine own native land remember me, for to me thou owest thy life."
>
> Then the wily Odysseus answered her:
>
> "Nausicaa, daughter of great-hearted Alcinous, may Zeus, the loud-thundering lord of Hera grant that I reach my home and see the day of my return. Then I will pray to thee as a god all my days, for thou, maiden, hast given me life." (8.454–468)

If Odysseus' rejection of Calypso's offer of immortality was a rejection of a sort of eternal and monotonous existence approximating death, the endless cycle of instinctive gratifications which left the spirit unsatisfied, his rejection of Nausicaa represents, paradoxically enough, his acceptance of a way of life which is more than mere existence. He now sees his own identity bound up with Penelope's. Away from home he is not himself.

I do not think it is doing violence to this crucial phase of the *Odyssey* to see in the Phaeacian visit a sort of spiritual and ideological revolution in the hero. This involves his reorientation in regard to the dominant values of the poem—the domestic and social values of which I have been speaking. Nor do I think it extravagant to insist that these values which center on the family, on the pre-eminent virtue of hospitality, and on the just administration of the state are shown throughout the poem as superior to what might be loosely designated as the heroic values of the *Iliad*. (In saying this I do not mean to imply that Homer gives unqualified assent to these values in the *Iliad*.) What threatens these domestic values is the old ideal of military glory and honor as man's noblest goal—the individualistic quest for eternal fame in battle. The *Odyssey* never disdains true honor as such, and in the slaughter of the suitors it recognizes that the most extreme punitive measures may sometimes be needed to protect society, but it submits what passes for honor to a searching inspection and shows that heroic deeds are often motivated by greed, accomplished with terror, and indistinguishable from piracy. In this poem Odysseus' career evolves from one set of values toward the other, from the narrow concepts of heroic honor to the broader concepts of the civilized man in a post-war world. Odysseus is not given to introspection, and his change of view is presented in a series of episodes that are emblematic of inner developments. Of these there are three main kinds: (1) a divine visitation; (2) an unexpected emotional response; and (3) a speech in which the hero analyzes his experiences in a way that lets us see implications of which he is only partly aware.

After his first meeting with Nausicaa on the shores of Phaeacia Athene transforms Odysseus, we are told, into a handsome man with hyacinthine locks. He has just bathed in the stream where Nausicaa and her maids have been doing the washing to rinse away "the scurf of the unresting sea." This bath is a spiritual as well as physical cleansing, for

> Athene the daughter of Zeus made him taller to look upon and mightier, and from his head she made the locks flow like hyacinth flowers. Just as when a smith overlays silver with gold, a cunning workman whom Hephaestus and Athene have taught all manner of craft, and his work is full of grace, even so the goddess shed grace upon his head and shoulders. Then he went apart and sat down on the shore gleaming with beauty and grace. (6.229–235)

The passage can of course be interpreted to some extent in purely naturalistic and psychological terms: Odysseus looks better after a bath and makes more of an impression on Nausicaa when duly washed and combed than did the uncouth and worn figure who emerged from the underbrush. But the fact that Athene is said to work this transformation is more than a mere *façon de parler,* for this is the first time, chronologically speaking, that she has had anything directly to do with her protégé in more than nine years. This miraculous change occurs at one other critical point in the poem, furthermore, and that is when Odysseus, having accomplished the destruction of the suitors and the purification of his halls, is transfigured before his meeting with Penelope. Both examples mark a rapprochement of the hero and his patroness, and the one under discussion signalizes Odysseus' reunion with all that Athene represents. It is important in this connection that Homer stresses Athene's role as patroness of domestic arts—that Arete and Penelope, for example, are said to be under her peculiar protection: "for Athene had given to them above all others skill in fair handiwork and an understanding heart" (7.110–111). It is even more important that the goddess of wisdom, whom the hero offended at Troy, gives at this point a particular mark of her favor.

Secondly, the fact that Homer has chosen Phaeacia as the setting for the hero's narration of what has happened to him in the last decade has more than structural significance. The peace-loving and hospitable Phaeacians who listen to his story serve as mute critics of his behavior. On the third day of his stay at Alcinous' court Odysseus asks the singer, Demodocus, to tell of his greatest exploit, the device of the wooden horse. There could be no more impressive build-up to revealing himself as the great "sacker of cities."

> "But come now, change thy theme and sing of the building of the wooden horse, which Epeius made with Athene's help, the horse which Odysseus once led up into the citadel as a thing of guile, when he had filled it with the men who sacked Ilios. If thou dost tell me this tale aright I will declare to all mankind that the god has with a willing heart granted thee the gift of divine song."
>
> . . . And he sang how the sons of the Achaeans poured forth from the horse and, leaving their hollow ambush, sacked the city. Of the others he sang how in various ways they wasted the high city, but of Odysseus, how he went like Ares to the

> house of Deiphobus together with godlike Menelaus. There it was, he said, that Odysseus braved the most terrible fight and in the end conquered by the aid of great-hearted Athene. (8.492–498; 514–520)

Odysseus reacts in a totally unexpected manner to this account of his exploits. His pride in his heroic accomplishments is suddenly transformed into pity for his victims. The moment of self-revelation is presented in a remarkable simile:

> And as a woman wails and flings herself about her dead husband who has fallen before his city and his people, seeking to ward off the pitiless day from his city and his children; and as she clings to him shrieking while the enemy behind her strike her back and shoulders with their spears and lead her to captivity to bear toil and woe, while her cheeks are wasted with most pitiful grief, even so did tears of pity fall from Odysseus' eyes. (523–531)

The moment of compassion includes for the first time those heretofore excluded from compassion on the grounds of being the "enemy." Until this moment the formalism of war prevented Odysseus from recognizing and feeling the humanity of his foes. Perhaps the effective man of war cannot afford too much imaginative and sympathetic identification with his victims, and must often pay for his effectiveness as a soldier by seeing the enemy as an abstraction or by denying them human status. This is what Odysseus has done up to this moment, and now all the sympathies suppressed or denied flood back upon him. The brutal side of heroic action is suddenly revealed in the question which the simile dramatically presents: does not the warrior's code destroy more than it creates? The question is raised elsewhere in the poem—by the disintegration of post-war Ithacan society under the lawless instincts liberated by the absence of the ruler, by the most sympathetic representation of enslaved or alienated or displaced people like Eumaeus, and by other dramatic incidents, pathetic, like this one, or ironic, like the question Polyphemus addresses to the tiny warriors in his cave: "Are you travelling on business or do you wander at random over the sea like pirates who risk their lives to bring evil to men of other lands?"—to which Odysseus answers proudly that he and his men are the followers of Agamemnon, whose fame is the greatest under heaven because of the city he sacked and the great numbers of people he killed.

The judgments which the *Odyssey* makes on the hero's behavior most often occur in this form. A community or an individual incorporates certain values beside which Odysseus is implicitly judged. Peripheral or minor characters are more frequently praised or condemned. Zeus himself expresses loathing for Aegisthus, and his attitude is reflected in the words of right-thinking characters such as Nestor, Telemachus, and Menelaus. Explicit evaluations of this third kind applied to Odysseus are so rare that they carry extraordinary force. An outstanding example is Circe's rebuke when Odysseus has angrily expressed his intention of defending his men against Scylla by force:

> "Rash man! Is thy heart still set on acts of war and on trouble? Wilt thou not yield even to the immortal gods? She is not mortal but an immortal bane, dreadful, sinister, fierce and not to be fought with. There is no defense; to flee from her is bravest." (12.116–120)

It is significant that Odysseus forgets this warning as he threads the straits and arms himself to the teeth without affecting the outcome. Circe's outburst exposes the excessive self-reliance which Odysseus must lose and does lose, as we have seen, before he is saved at Phaeacia from his long battle with the sea.

Even less frequent is the self-critical, introspective speech. In his autobiographical narrative Odysseus does not consciously relate his behavior over the past ten years to any principles, moral or otherwise. We find in his account examples of unregulated pride, brutality, and lust among moments of vision and restraint, and they are defined as such by the religious, social and political idyll of Phaeacia, as well as by the principle of contrast in the individual adventures. Though Odysseus never sums up with a *mea culpa,* he emerges from the telling at harmony with himself and with human, natural, and supernatural elements of his universe. The final stamp of approval on the rehabilitation he has undergone is given in his reunion with Athene in Book Thirteen. Here he meets his divine protectress undisguised and face-to-face for the first time since the fall of Troy. His words at this moment verge on the analytical, moral judgment:

> It is hard, goddess, for a mortal however wise to know thee, for thou changest thy shape at will. But this I know well—that long ago, while we were fighting at Troy, thou wast kind

> to me. But when we had sacked Priam's towering city, and had gone away in our ships, and a god had scattered the Achaeans, I have never seen thee since, daughter of Zeus, nor marked thee boarding my vessel to ward off sorrow from me. (13.312–319)

One short step further and Odysseus would realize the connection between his past acts and the alienation of Athene. *We* realize it, but Homer prefers the dramatic to the analytical method.

This moment of reunion marks the beginning of Odysseus' role as judge and restorer of Ithaca. The goddess who left him when he sacked her shrine at Troy watches over him throughout the greatest of all his enterprises. Odysseus plays his part through most of the second half of the poem not as a king or a warrior but in the disguise of an abject old beggar. The significance of this disguise is almost inexhaustible. It enables him to test the charity of the suitors, and charity is one of the essential virtues in the world of the *Odyssey*. It suggests the fundamental weakness of all men and their dependence on their brothers. It dramatizes divine immanence in human affairs in accordance with the idea that the gods often take upon themselves the basest and poorest human shapes. It is a further demonstration that human worth is not graded according to rank or position or power. It represents the theme that all men are beggars, outcasts, and wanderers in some sense at one time or another, a theme that is traced through the fugitive Theoclymenus and such displaced persons as Eurycleia and Eumaeus. It is, finally, a test of Odysseus' own inner strength—his patience and self-restraint. As Odysseus experiences the insults and cruelties of some of the suitors and some of his own servants, as he witnesses from the depths of his own experience the blasphemous frivolity of Antinous and Eurymachus, he imposes on himself the hardest task of all for such a passionate and action-loving nature. He holds his peace and leaves the satisfaction of his cause to be determined by the gods. As the beggar who continually appeals to the suitors for alms in the name of Zeus, to whom strangers and refugees are sacred, and in the name of common humanity, which unites men in the experiences of hunger, vicissitude, and humiliation, he displays a courage more difficult for him and more valuable for civilization than he did in the wooden horse. When Ctesippus hits him with the cow's hoof, or Antinous throws a stool at him, he stands "firm as a rock . . . shaking his head in silence, and pondering evil in the deep of his heart." In the midst of these provocations to violence he remains just and does all in his power to save some of the better men among the suitors by appeals to their wisdom and sense of justice. Amphinomous has shown him charity, and Odysseus' plea to him is the most explicit statement in the *Odyssey* of a moral theme and at the same time Odysseus' clearest evaluation of his own experience:

> Of all things that breathe and move on the face of the earth there is none feebler than man. For he thinks that he will never suffer evil in time to come as long as the gods give him prosperity and his knees are strong; but when the blessed gods decree sorrow for him he bears it reluctantly with an enduring spirit, for our outlook on earth depends on the day to day fortunes which the father of gods and men brings upon us. For I too once prospered among men, but I did many wicked deeds, yielding to my strength and trusting in the power of my father and brothers. Therefore let no man ever be lawless, but let him keep silently whatever gifts the gods give. (18.130–142)

This shift from power, which is accidental, to the principle of justice, which is in the reach of every man, marks the extraordinary moral revolution which occurs in the *Odyssey* and in the character of its hero. Without this principle the best that life has to offer is "the human and personal tragedy built up against the background of meaningless flux," which C. S. Lewis wrongly finds in the *Odyssey* as well as the *Iliad*. The power and excitement I find in the *Odyssey* stem in large measure from its testimony to the birth of civilization in the emergence of charity and law and order out of the flux of passion and aimless brutality.

If one thinks of the *Odyssey* as the rehabilitation of a veteran after a long and terrible war in the course of which the justice of the cause has been betrayed, as is so often the case, by the methods of the crusaders; if one sees the hero's long voyage home as an exploration of his identity as man; if one feels that he cannot arrive home in the profoundest sense until he has discovered the metaphysical order of the human community, the deepest significance of this great poem will not, I am convinced, be violated. The historical circumstances of Odysseus' situation are so like ours that his restoration of the waste land within and outside him has the deepest relevance for ourselves.

IV

The Name of Odysseus

GEORGE E. DIMOCK, JR.

"There is no way to stand firm on both feet and escape trouble." *Odyssey* 5.413–414

IN A WAY, the whole problem of the *Odyssey* is for Odysseus to establish his identity. "After all, who knows who his father is?" says Telemachus in the first book. "My son, if he really ever existed," says Laertes in the last. To establish his identity Odysseus must live up to his name.

This is not a new idea. A nameless ancient commentator has puzzled editors by glossing *hēbēsas* in line 410 of the nineteenth book with *odyssamenos. Hēbēsas* means "when he has grown up," a meaning with which *odyssamenos* has nothing to do; but as we shall see, the scholiast means that for Odysseus to grow up, to achieve his full stature, will be for him to "odysseus"—to live up to the meaning of his name, whatever that may be.

"To odysseus" (*odyssasthai* in Greek) is usually said to mean "be wroth against," "hate," and to be connected with Latin *odisse*. Historically speaking, this may be true. For the *Odyssey*'s poetical purposes, however, the verb denotes a more general sort of hostility, which Homer is at pains to define. In the fifth book the nymph Ino explains it as "planting evils," without specifying what sort of hostility is in the mind of the planter. It is true that Poseidon, who happens to be the planter in this case, is angry; but Zeus, who also odysseuses

Reprinted by permission from *The Hudson Review,* IX (Spring, 1956), 52–70.

Odysseus, is not. In the nineteenth book Odysseus' grandfather Autolycus indicates that it is not a question of anger; asked to name the baby, he replies,

> "I have odysseused many in my time, up and down the wide world, men and women both; therefore let his name be Odysseus."

Now, all we know from the *Odyssey* about Autolycus' career is that he was the foremost liar and thief of his day. Most naturally, by "odysseusing many" he means that he has been the bane of many people's existence. The secret of his palpable success would seem to be that he has never given a sucker an even break, and he wants his grandson to be like him. In the career of Autolycus, and in the attitude which it implies, we are much closer to the *polytropon* "crafty" of the *Odyssey*'s first line, than to the *mēnin* "wrath" of the *Iliad*'s. So let us think no more of "wrath," which implies provocation and mental perturbation, but rather of a hand and mind against every man, by nature, or as a matter of policy. Autolycus' own name does not suggest "Lone Wolf" for nothing. These considerations, and others, lead me to think that in the *Odyssey odyssasthai* means essentially "to cause pain (*odynē*), and to be willing to do so." We need not draw the line between subjective and objective here, any more than we need do so in the case of the word "suffer." Where did Odysseus "suffer" the "woes" of the *Odyssey*'s fourth line: "on the high seas," or "in his heart"? Just as "suffer" brings to mind both the external and internal aspects of being a victim, so "odysseus" implies subjectively and objectively what it is to persecute. For what it is worth, the seven-odd instances of the verb outside the *Odyssey* show nothing inconsistent with this meaning.

Autolycus, then, we discover in the nineteenth book, intended Odysseus to be a causer of pain. He has been one all along, of course. Perhaps the most prominent fact about him is that more than any other man he was responsible for taking Troy; and what it means to sack a city, we know from the simile at the end of Book Eight. Odysseus

> wept as a woman weeps when she throws her arms around the body of her beloved husband, fallen in battle before his city and his comrades, fighting to save his town and his children from

> disaster. She has found him gasping in the throes of death; she clings to him and lifts her voice in lamentation. But the enemy come up and belabor her back and shoulders with spears, as they lead her off into slavery and a life of miserable toil, with her cheeks wasted by her pitiful grief.[1]

Less than a hundred lines later, at the beginning of his tale, Odysseus will say,

> The same wind as wafted me from Ilium brought me to Ismarus, the city of the Cicones; I sacked the place and killed the men; their wives, together with much booty, we took out of the city and divided up.

As has been well observed, the Sack of Ismarus is the Sack of Troy in its predatory essentials, with the glamor stripped off. This attitude Odysseus will maintain to the end. "The cattle which the suitors have consumed," he says in the twenty-third book, "I will for the most part make up by raiding on my own; the Achaeans will give others." Perhaps worse than this, Odysseus' going to Troy caused Telemachus grievous mental suffering, wasted Penelope's nights in tears, and reduced Laertes, his father, to misery and squalor; his absence killed his mother, Anticleia.

So conceived, Odysseus is not an attractive character. In fact the poem implies a good deal of criticism of the Autolycan attitude. As Mr. H. N. Porter once pointed out to me, one of the first things we hear about the hero is his predilection for poisoned arrows. Athene, disguised as Mentes, tells Telemachus,

> He was on his way from Ephyre, where he had stayed with Ilus Mermerides—he went there in his fast ship to get a mortal poison to smear his bronze-tipped arrows with. Ilus wouldn't give it to him in fear of the eternal gods. But my father [Zeus?] gave him some. He was terribly fond of him.

Much better, one would think, for Autolycus to have adopted Eurycleia's suggestion of Polyaretus as a name for the baby: "He's our 'Answer to Prayer' (*polyarētos*)," she remarked as she put the child on his grandfather's lap. But Autolycus preferred a name that most would regard as ill-omened.

For in spite of the fact that Odysseus is so obviously a causer of pain, the name which Autolycus wished on him strikes one as ironical. Up to the nineteenth book, Odysseus has been referred to as odysseused rather than odysseusing: "Why do you odysseus him so, Zeus?" Athene asks, before the poem is well under way; Ino and Odysseus both say that Poseidon is odysseusing him; finally, as we read the Autolycus passage, we are aware that Odysseus has just told Penelope that Zeus and the Sun-god odysseused her husband. In the *Odyssey's* proem itself, the hero seems essentially the sufferer: he is the *polytropos* man, the Autolycan rogue who treats the world as his enemy, but who sacks Troy only to be driven far astray thereafter, and take a beating. In the process, we are told, he is to win his *psychē,* which means loosely his life, and more properly the image of life after the liver is gone—in other words something very like identity—but the whole business seems unpleasant, to say the least.

To understand the satisfaction involved in injuring and suffering and the connection between them, we must return to the nineteenth book and the scholiast's note. The giving of the name is coupled with the adventure in which Odysseus first lives up to it. *Hēbēsas* is in fact *odyssamenos.* "When he has grown up," the hero, as though undergoing an initiation, wins Autolycus' favor and recognition by going on a boar hunt; as causer of pain he kills the boar; as sufferer he is slashed by it, thus acquiring the scar important in identifying him later. The pain given and received results in joy:

> Autolycus and the sons of Autolycus
> Efficiently healed him and loaded him with presents;
> Rejoicing they dispatched him rejoicing to his beloved
> Ithaca. His father and his good mother
> Rejoiced at his return, and asked for each particular
> Of how he got his scar.

The suffering results from the doing, and is inseparable from it in the recognition and satisfaction produced by this exploit. Not simply "how he killed the boar" but "how he got his scar," is for Odysseus' parents the measure of their son.

To be Odysseus, then, is to adopt the attitude of the hunter of dangerous game: to deliberately expose one's self, but thereafter to take every advantage that the exposed position admits; the immediate purpose is injury, but the ultimate purpose is recognition and the sense of a great exploit. Odysseus killed a boar to win his name; he went to Troy to enlarge it; in order to keep it, he will presently kill 108 suitors in as cold blood as he can manage.

In the adventure with the Cyclops, Odysseus inflicts pain in order to identify himself, and in so doing challenges the hostility of the universe. Polyphemus' pain is obvious. Even Euripides could not have dwelt more explicitly than Homer on the boring of the red-hot stake into the great eyeball, the sizzling of the eye's fluid, and the crackling of its roots. By virtue of this deed of horror, Odysseus, until now *Outis* "nobody" as far as Polyphemus is concerned, puts himself in a position where he can tell the monster who he is, can cry his name aloud to the Cyclops' face. This cry of defiance is thought to be foolish of the wily Odysseus, no less by his crew than by the critics, but it is in reality, like the boar hunt, a case of deliberate self-exposure for the purpose of being somebody rather than nobody.

To blind the son of Poseidon, and then to defy him, is both to challenge nature to do her worst, and to demonstrate her ultimate impotence to crush human identity. It is challenging nature in the sense that the sailor does, every time he goes to sea. The hero's colonizing eye as he approaches the Cyclopes' island, the remark that they have no ships or shipwrights, the shipbuilding technique employed in blinding Polyphemus and the mention of axe, adze and auger, the tools which enabled Odysseus to leave Calypso and set sail on his raft, all this sounds very much as though Odysseus' crime against Poseidon were the crime of all those who go down to the sea in ships. But Poseidon will not get his revenge. In the *Odyssey* navigation is a practical possibility; the elements are conquered. So to blind Polyphemus is to convict savage nature of impotence and blindness. She is indiscriminate in her blows. Her most hostile efforts, like the rocks thrown by Polyphemus, are as likely to wash the hero to safety as they are to drive him into danger. Thus the power of the elements does not render Odysseus' identity meaningless. Rather he makes sense, and the elements do not. This, I think, is the significance of the general assumption in the *Odyssey* that Poseidon will give Odysseus his bellyful of trouble before he reaches his home, but will not kill him.

Polyphemus and Poseidon, however, are more than the hostility of inanimate nature. There is no "inanimate nature" in Homer anyway. They prefigure all the overt savagery which the universe presents, human and divine. This savagery is as able to breach the conventions, hospitality and the rest, among the civilized suitors in Ithaca, or the hypercivilized Phaeacians (remember Euryalus), as it is among the cannibal Laestrygonians, or among the Cyclopes. If Poseidon and Polyphemus are the hostile aspects of this world, it is not foolish for Odysseus to cry his name in defiance of them, and so be subject to Polyphemus' rock-slinging and his curse; or rather, the foolishness or good sense of the action is not the point. To pass from the darkness of the cave into the light, to pass from being "nobody" to having a name, is to be born. But to be born is to cast one's name in the teeth of a hostile universe; it is to incur the enmity of Poseidon. In such a world, what better name could be found than Odysseus, "Trouble"? ("Trouble" is perhaps as good a translation of Odysseus' name as any. When a character in a western movie says, "Just call me Trouble, stranger," we take him to be a hostile type who makes trouble for other people, and so presumably for himself also.)

That braving Polyphemus is being born is not my metaphor; it is Homer's. In the nineteenth book Odysseus hints to Penelope that her husband has undergone a birth somewhere overseas:

> He put in at Amnisus, where the cave of Eileithuia is, in a difficult harbor; he barely escaped the gales.

Eileithuia is goddess of childbirth. But in the nineteenth book this is merely a way of reminding us of the Polyphemus adventure and possibly of Calypso as well. In the ninth book, as Polyphemus is in the act of rolling the stone from the mouth of the cave, we are told of his anguish for the second time. We already know how his eye hurts, but this time we hear that he is "travailing in pain"; *ōdinōn odynēsi* are the words used. Whether or not we hear in them the name of Odysseus, we should not fail to reflect that *ōdinō* means essentially "to be in labor of childbirth." We are born for trouble, the adventure of the Cyclops implies, yet to stay in the womb is to remain nobody. There is security of a sort in being nobody, but as the Cyclops promises, Nobody will be devoured in the end, though last of all.

For there are more insidious threats to identity in the *Odyssey* than those which Polyphemus represents, the dangers and sufferings consequent upon taking on the world as one's enemy. Trouble is difficult and dangerous, but it can lead to identity. Security, on the other hand, is inevitable oblivion. The narrative proper of the *Odyssey* begins as follows:

> By now all the others, as many as had escaped sheer destruction, were at home. Odysseus, alone of all, wanting his home and his wife, a queenly nymph held prisoner, Calypso, divine goddess, in her hollow cave, begging him to be her husband.

This is the state of affairs which the fifth book will develop. He wants home and a wife. He has a cave and a goddess. Why do all the gods but one pity him for this? Odysseus has realized the tired soldier's or sailor's dream, an immortality of comfort and physical satisfaction, with no troubles. But Odysseus would rather die, as Athene says. Everybody sees this paradox and understands the flaw in this paradise: such an existence has no meaning. But it adds something, I think, to see life on Ogygia in terms of identity and nonentity. Calypso is oblivion. Her name suggests cover and concealment, or engulfing; she lives "in the midst of the sea"—the middle of nowhere, as Hermes almost remarks—and the whole struggle of the fifth book, indeed of the entire poem, is not to be engulfed by that sea. When the third great wave of Book Five breaks over Odysseus' head, Homer's words are: *ton de mega kyma kalypsen*—"and the great wave engulfed him." If this wave had drowned him, it would have been a "vile death," surely, as Odysseus remarks at the beginning of the storm. Much better, he says, to have died where "the spears flew thickest" at Troy; then he would have had "recognition," *kleos*. People would know about him and his death. Odysseus does not wish he were back with Calypso. Though she offered immortality, not death—an immortality of security and satisfaction in a charming cave—it is still an immortality of oblivion, of no *kleos,* of nonentity. Leaving Calypso is very like leaving the perfect security and satisfaction of the womb; but, as the Cyclops reminds us, the womb is after all a deadly place. In the womb one has no identity, no existence worthy of a name. Nonentity and identity are in fact the poles between which the actors in the poem move. It is a choice between Scylla and Charybdis—to face deliberately certain trouble from the jaws of the six-headed goddess, or to be engulfed entirely by the maelstrom. One must odysseus and be odysseused, or else be kalypsoed.

Odysseus did not always live up to his name. There was one occasion when oblivion seemed almost preferable to trouble. His name seemd to have lost its magic. Hence his failure with the Laestrygonians, and the necessity of winning back his identity in the Circe episode.

While we remember Polyphemus ("Much-fame") in connection with Odysseus, we are very apt to forget Antiphates ("Against-renown"), the Laestrygonian king. In the Laestrygonian affair Odysseus himself avoids the encounter, and loses his whole fleet. In this, his least creditable adventure, he never makes his identity felt. The Laestrygonians don't know who he is, or care. Yet Odysseus survives. With poetic rather than nautical logic, he escapes by virtue of having left his ship in an exposed position, while the rest of the fleet trusts itself to the security of the fiord and is lost.

Odysseus in the land of the Laestrygonians is not the Odysseus whom we saw with the Cyclops, though in both cases he has to do with cannibal giants. Avoiding the encounter here is perhaps as sensible as avoiding the Planctae, but there are other reasons why Odysseus is not up to it. In the interim, as we have said, his name has lost its magic. "Trouble," intended to mean success, has seemed to be failure. Aeolus has listened with interest to the tale of prowess at Troy and has sent Odysseus on his way, insuring that he will have, for once, a remarkably painless trip. But in sight of the goal, trouble strikes. Aeolus, seeing in this a sign that heaven is inveterately hostile to Odysseus, banishes him from his sight. Such trouble means to Aeolus not identity, but oblivion. Odysseus himself has nearly reached a similar conclusion. Since leaving Troy he has sacked Ismarus in characteristically ruthless fashion and rejected the passive peace of Lotus-land. By handling the situation in a manner worthy of Autolycus, he has been able to cry his name in defiance of Polyphemus. He has come within sight of his home. He has done all this only to find his achievement undone at the first relaxation of his mistrustful watchfulness. Small wonder that success on these terms should seem impossible. As the winds sped Odysseus out of sight of Ithaca, "I debated," he says, "whether to leap from my ship and end it all in the sea" (embracing thus the "vile death" of the Calypso episode), "or whether to bear my misery and remain among the living." He adopts a sort of compromise: "I endured and I remained; *kalypsamenos* I lay in my ship," he puts it, meaning that he had wrapped his head in his cloak. This is the Odysseus who fails to confront Antiphates.

After the discouragement of the Aeolus episode, it is natural that life's difficulties should appear as insuperable as the Laestrygonians; but Odysseus will find the courage to go on. After the Laestrygonian experience his depression is shared by his men. Two days they all lie in weariness and woe on Circe's beach. But against this sea of troubles Odysseus takes arms, a spear and a sword. As he once killed a boar, he now kills a stag. This puts heart in Odysseus' men: "dis-kalypsoed" (*ek de kalypsamenoi*) they revive. Odysseus now makes a remarkable speech:

> Friends, we don't know where the darkness is, or where the dawn; where the sun that shines for mortals rises, or where it sets. Still let us quickly consider whether any resource can still be found. I for one don't think so.

The point, as Odysseus goes on to suggest, is whether they must indeed make themselves known and ask the inhabitants of the island for their route, perilous though it has proved to confront Polyphemus and Antiphates. In other words, shall they turn their backs on the comparative security of their present oblivion? Characteristically, this wider implication is stressed by a pun—a blatant pun which has been used before, in the Cyclops passage. "Whether any resource can still be found," sounds in Greek almost precisely like "Whether any of us is going to go on being nobody." "I for one don't think so," is Odysseus' comment. They have been "nobody" for some time, in fact ever since Aeolus refused to recognize their claims as human beings. This cannot go on, as the pun implies. The time has come when Odysseus must stand and be recognized.

Without taking account of the pun, critics have interpreted this passage as Odysseus at the end of his human resources, about to apply for divine aid. The moly plant, soon to be granted, becomes for them almost a symbol of grace. This is fair enough in its way. Identity in the Odyssey is in some sense a gift of the gods. But "from the gods who sit in grandeur, grace comes somehow violent."[2] Odysseus doesn't pray for grace; he exacts it, first by killing the stag and then by threatening Circe and forcing her to swear to do him no harm. Hermes, Autolycus' patron, puts him up to the threatening, but it is quite in accord with Odysseus' name and nature anyhow. We remember the oaths exacted from Helen and Calypso. In the present instance Odysseus remains nobody, a denatured wolf or lion like Circe's other victims, until sword to throat, he makes her recognize him and speak his name. Prior to this, despite the introductory formula "he took my hand and spoke my name," Hermes had not named the hero; he only named his passive aspect, *O dystēne* "poor wretch." But with the gift of moly, "black at the root, but with a flower like milk," Hermes seems to restore the magic of the name of Odysseus. However black its first effects, it will ultimately flower with balm and solace. Though she "struck [him] with her rod and named" him, Circe gives Odysseus no name at all until the hero seems "like one eager to kill her"; once having recognized him as "Odysseus *polytropos*" however, she uses his name every chance she gets, four times with full titles: "Zeus-sprung son of Laertes, expedient Odysseus." By choosing to live up to his name with Circe, Odysseus restored its magic; he had to in order to get anywhere, and so to be anybody, at all.

For Odysseus to choose to pursue the path of his painful identity as he did on Circe's beach, is to win power over, and recognition from, that ambiguous daughter of Sun, the life-giver, and Ocean, the all-engulfing. It is also to accept pain as the only real basis of meaning in this life or the next. This is the secret of Teiresias.

To achieve the goal of recognition and identity, and to learn the secrets of the abyss, are equally to row upon the sea of trouble. This is the meaning of the apparently witless question, "What ship brought you to Ithaca, for I do not think you came on foot," and of Anticleia's first words to her son in the underworld:

> My child, how did you come beneath the misty dark, alive as you are? It is hard for the living to get a sight of all this. For in between are great rivers and dreadful streams, first Ocean, which there is no way to cross on foot, if one does not have a well-built ship.

But with Aeolus the question arose, is such sea-faring endurable? To ask this question is "to enquire of Teiresias" (*Teiresiēs* in

Homer); for Teiresias' name is the weariness of rowing. *"TEIReto d' andrōn thymos hyp' EIRESIĒS alegeinēs,"* Odysseus says of his crew after Aeolus denied them: *"Worn* was my men's spirit by the woeful *rowing."* To enquire of Teiresias is to ask the meaning of trouble.

This is why Odysseus is not so much interested in what the prophet has to say of the troubled future—"You seek homecoming sweet as honey, noble Odysseus; heaven will make it hard for you"—as he is in recognition, in the meaning of his own painful and pain-producing existence:

> Doubtless the gods had all that in store for me. But tell me: I see here the shade of my dead mother; she sits in silence near the blood, and has not the strength to look her son in the face or speak to him. Tell me, lord, how might she recognize the man I am?

His mother's recognition contains a blow. It was Odysseus' sweet nature, she says, that killed her. Thus it appears that even in his gentlest aspect, Odysseus gives pain. He is, after all, soft as well as hard. The predatory brooch, dog throttling fawn, pinned on him by Penelope as he left for Troy, is coupled with a second mark of identification, equally important: the shirt which gleamed on his body

> like the skin of a dried onion—so gentle it was to the touch, and at the same time bright, like the sun; many were the women who admired it.

Yet Odysseus' soft side can be as painful, or as fatal, as his hardness. The love, not the hate he inspired, killed the dog Argus and wasted Penelope's nights in tears. Anticleia recognized at least part of her son's nature by dying for the love of him.

Agamemnon, dead by no sweet nature, but rather by the treacherous hand of his wife, also recognizes Odysseus; despite Penelope's virtue, he had better not, Agamemnon thinks in contrast to Anticleia, tell his wife everything. Neither of these recognitions, neither the first, evoking the hero's sweetness, nor the second, calling upon his guile, can bring Odysseus much comfort as to the value of life as Trouble. Achilles on the other hand makes it clear that it is something to be alive at all, and furthermore his concern for his son's prowess reminds us that Telemachus, too, promises to become a credit to his father. Still, neither simple existence, nor existence continued through a worthy son, is of the essence. Ajax' silence, though eloquently expressive of the power of Odysseus as injurer, is discouraging; but the climax of recognition is reached when Heracles, whose "seeming" is hell's own picture of hostile ferocity, but whose reality "dwells in bliss among the immortals," equates Odysseus to himself:

> One look was enough to tell Heracles who I was, and he greeted me in mournful tones. "Zeus-sprung son of Laertes, expedient Odysseus—unhappy man! So you too are working out some such miserable doom as I was slave to when the sun shone over my head. Son of Zeus though I was, unending troubles came my way. . . . a master far beneath my rank . . . sent me down here to bring away the Hound of Hell. And under the guiding hands of Hermes and bright-eyed Athene, I did succeed in capturing him and I dragged him out of Hades' realm."

Not just Heracles, but all these people (except Ajax) explicitly recognize Odysseus; still excepting Ajax, all but Anticleia, who appropriately calls him "my child," use Odysseus' full titles. Each sees him differently, and to a greater or less degree, truly. To all of them he means, in one way or another, pain. To Anticleia he is the pain of a lost child; Agamemnon connects him with the pain and betrayal that marriage may bring; Achilles is reminded of the ultimate pain of being dead, Ajax of wounded honor. Heracles sees in him the "unending troubles" of life under the sun. For the secret of life which Odysseus has come to the realms of the dead to discover is the necessity of pain, and its value. The generations of woman ("and each proclaimed her bringing-forth") may be for good or ill, involving Zeus or Poseidon indifferently. Man's fate may seem to be Tantalus' endless craving, never satisfied; or Sisyphus' endless striving, never successful; life's basis may even be Tityus' vultures, a great gnawing in a great belly, as Odysseus several times suggests (7.216–221; 15.343–344; 17.286–289; 18.53–54). Yet Minos continues to pass his judgments, and Orion to pursue his quarry. Heracles has his heavenly, as well as his hellish aspect—and so does Odysseus, "Trouble." Ajax feels only Odysseus' hellish side, but Heracles implies that a life of pain, given and received, snatches something from Death himself. This is the secret of Teiresias, the answer to the weariness of rowing. To know himself as Trouble, and to be so known by others, is the only way for Odysseus to possess his identity.

There is no human identity in other terms than pain. To escape Calypso, Odysseus needs a ship (4.559–560; 5.16–17), and so must accept the weariness of rowing. To see life in any other way is to live in a dream-world, as the Cyclopes do, and the Phaeacians. To avoid trouble, the Phaeacians withdrew, we are told, from their ancestral conflict with the Cyclopes. The conflict is indeed ancestral, for the Cyclopes are as savage as the Phaeacians are civilized; but both are out of touch with reality. Polyphemus thinks he can act with impunity, "for we are much mightier than the gods," but he succumbs to Trouble in the shape of a clever "weakling" and a skin of wine. The Phaeacians on the contrary trust in their piety. Nausicaa thinks that no one could possibly come "bringing enmity, for we are dear to the gods." This she says of Odysseus, Enmity himself. To her, he is either an object of pity or a dream come true:

> Doubtless she has picked up some castaway from his ship [she thinks of someone as remarking of her], a foreign man, since there is nobody like that nearby [or "those nearby are nobodies"], or else in answer to her hopes a god, long prayed-for (*polyarētos*), has come down from heaven to keep her all her days.

Eurycleia's "Polyaretus" fits Odysseus in the sense that his return to Ithaca in his hostile might is something to pray for, but he is not what Nausicaa would pray that he be. Nausicaa is victimized by her too trusting love for him, and his visit is ultimately disastrous for her people. The *Odyssey* has its dream-worlds, and, "near to the gods," Scheria is one of them. Its queen, "whose name is Prayed-for" (*Arētē d'onom' estin epōnymon*), suggests her antonym, Odysseus, who, the poem later tells us, might have been Polyaretus, but was not. "So let his name be Trouble" (*to d' Odysseus onom' estin epōnymon*), Autolycus will say in the nineteenth book.

Odysseus no more can exist in the dream-world of Alcinous and Arete, where woman rules man and rowing is no trouble, than he can with Calypso. In a world without trouble love must be as little serious as the affair of Ares and Aphrodite. With Nausicaa there is no scope for the relationship which Odysseus describes to her:

> There is nothing nobler or more admirable than when two people who see eye to eye keep house as man and wife, *confounding their enemies* and delighting their friends, as they themselves know better than anyone.

How can love be really felt, without pain? Therefore, after arriving exhausted, naked, and unknown on Scheria, Odysseus must somehow so impress the inhabitants that they will send him on his way, neither killing him as enemy nor overmuch befriending him and settling him down with Nausicaa. This he accomplishes primarily by means of his well-advertised Tale of Woe. It is received with mingled horror and fascination. Avid for its miseries the Phaeacians certainly are. This supports our impression that their dream-world, lacking pain, is human life *manqué*. On the other hand, after the simile of the woman led into captivity, it is easy to assume Phaeacian feelings of horror at Odysseus' brutal account of the Sack of Ismarus. The recognition accorded the tale is equivocal: "Phaeacians," Arete asks during the intermission, "what do you think of this man, his size and strength and wit?" A dubious answer is implied in Alcinous' polite comment:

> O Odysseus, when we look at you we don't find you a bit like a liar and thief, [or "your *Outis* looks to us like a liar and thief"] such as the black earth produces in such far-flung numbers—thieves piling lie on lie, and where they get them all from nobody knows; your words are charming, there is good sense in them, and you tell your story as skillfully as a bard, the grim sufferings of yourself and all the Argives.

After all Odysseus has shown himself to be a pirate, and it is worth noting that Alcinous' remarks occur half-way through the story of the underworld, before the value of pain is established. But for the Phaeacians this is never established. Their rowing is without drudgery, for all their sea-faring. At the end of the tale Alcinous will tell the guest he once thought of as a son-in-law that he is sure he will never come back. One doesn't quite know whether the Phaeacians are bestowing on Odysseus more wealth than he won at Troy in recognition of his exploits, or as an invitation to leave the country; for it was Odysseus' stated willingness to stay a year that brought forth Alcinous' remarks about liars and thieves. In Odysseus the

Phaeacians enjoy Trouble vicariously, but ultimately dismiss him. We may be pretty sure that, for their "painless escorting of strangers," Poseidon's threat to "surround (*amphikalypsai*) their city with mountains" will come off. Just as he turned their ship to stone, he will bar them from the sea, and therefore from any chance of future identity. The price of no trouble is oblivion.

Teiresias implies three modes of pain: first, pain administered, like the slaying of the boar and stag, or the blinding of Polyphemus. Odysseus, Teiresias predicts, will kill the suitors. Second, there is the pain of the resisted impulse. Odysseus must restrain his predatory impulses when he comes upon the cattle of the Sun. Third, to plant the oar, the symbol of the weariness of rowing, among those "who do not know the sea, nor eat their food mixed with salt, nor know of red-prowed ships, nor balanced oars, which are a vessel's wings" is to introduce the idea of trouble to those who, like the Phaeacians, are not sufficiently aware of it. In establishing his identity, Odysseus must use these three modes of pain.

It is sufficiently clear how administering pain by killing the suitors and threatening their kinsmen with annihilation serves to establish Odysseus in Ithaca. The second mode is subtler. It would seem a denial of Odysseus' name for him to boggle at a little cattle-rustling. That he does so leads some to suppose that his adventures are intended to purge him of the brutalizing effects of the Trojan campaign and bring him home readjusted to civilian life. But the temptation of the cattle of the Sun is more like the temptation of the Lotus than like the Sack of Ismarus. It is a temptation not to crime but to oblivion. To fall for it is the typical weakness of the "innocent" crew, as the proem suggests. Faced with the Planctae, the Reefs of Hard Knocks, they drop their oars. Knowing the mortal danger in eating the Sun's cattle, they do not know it thoroughly enough to forgo the immediate satisfaction of eating when they are hungry. Forgetful of homecoming and identity itself, they eat. Of all that band only Odysseus can resist such impulses and hang on interminably, as he does clinging to the fig tree above Charybdis, refusing to drop and be comfortably engulfed.

Odysseus is a master of the delayed response, of the long way round, of the resisted impulse. That is the reason he is able to keep his identity intact. It is courting oblivion to rush blindly into love, as Nausicaa did, and as Penelope, even when reunited with her husband, did not. In Circe's bed, Odysseus would have become just another denatured wolf or lion, if he had not first with a show of hostility made sure of his integrity. As in love, so with eating. Man is a predatory animal; to eat he must kill; but he must know what he is doing. He must not, like the crew and the suitors, take life as a table spread before him, insufficiently aware of the presence of enemies.

He must not even take life as a song, though the episode of the Sirens suggests that this is the most irresistible of impulses. The Phaeacians are certainly not proof against it. Alcinous may think that the meaning of life's pain is that

> the gods were responsible for that, weaving catastrophe into the pattern of events to make a song for future generations,

but pain must be experienced, not just enjoyed as after-dinner entertainment. Therefore the Phaeacians are victimized by Odysseus' Tale of Woe. Odysseus on the other hand is proof against the Sirens and their singing of "all things that happen on this fruitful earth," just as he is against the Lotus and against Circe. He is steadfast in enduring Teiresias' second mode of pain, the pain of the resisted impulse.

"The steadfast," says a priest in *Murder in the Cathedral,* "can manipulate the greed and lust of others, the feeble is devoured by his own." This leads us from the second mode of pain to the third—introducing the idea of trouble to those insufficiently aware of it. Odysseus in his steadfastness knows the pain of the thirst for life, the danger it leads to, and the trouble involved in successfully gratifying it. He knows it so well ("he saw the cities of many men, and knew their mind"), that he can use this knowledge in manipulating others, for the purpose of getting himself recognized as Trouble. One picture of this is Odysseus in the underworld, sword in hand, controlling the access of the ghosts to the blood. Manipulating the Phaeacians chiefly through their itching ears, he introduces himself to them as Trouble, and wins survival and homecoming. In the second half of the poem, using his lying tales, his wife, and the good things of his house as bait, he maneuvers the upholders and the defilers of his household alike into a position where, bow in hand and arrow on string, like Heracles in the underworld, he can make himself really felt.

For Odysseus to establish his identity at home, manipulation is necessary, manipulation even of those who favor him. It is difficult to get people to accept pain. Even the suitors do not dispute that he was a good king; unfortunately this is not enough to maintain his position in Ithaca. He must get both his pleasant and his hostile aspect recognized at the same time. When they finally are, near the end of the last book, this is signalized by the curious salutation of Dolius, the last to join forces with him: *oule te kai mala chaire,* he says, "hail and rejoice!" But *oule* is an exceedingly rare word, and its auditory suggestions of *oulos* "baneful," and *oulē,* the famous scar, will be felt—something like "Bane and Weal!" For the scar which the boar gave him is in particular the mark of Odysseus as Trouble. Anticleia ("Opposed-to-fame"), in her recognition of her son in the underworld, did not seem to understand the scar's full meaning, but it is easy for Eurycleia ("Far-fame") to accept it. After touching the scar as she washed his feet,

> joy and pain seized upon Eurycleia at the same time; her eyes filled with tears, and the voice caught in her throat. Touching his chin she said to Odysseus: "Surely you are Odysseus, dear child—and I didn't know my master until I had felt all of him!"

Eurycleia knows both aspects. It is she who has to be restrained from howling in triumph over the dead suitors. Telemachus is not much of a problem either. "I am no god;" Odysseus says, "Why do you think I am an immortal? No, I am your father, for whom you groan and suffer so much pain, accepting the insults of your fellows." Telemachus' difficulty is to determine whether Trouble is a miserable wretch in filthy rags or a very god for splendor. We have met this ambiguity before in the double nature of Heracles.

Penelope's recognition is harder to win. She knows Odysseus' soft garment, and her own hands pinned on him the badge of the dog and fawn; but the predatory side of him she cannot accept. Troy is to her not a great and necessary exploit, but something he merely "went to see," and for this she cannot forgive him. To her Troy is not a source of renown, but "Evil Ilium, not to be named." If Odysseus' manipulation, or his knowledge of the mind of man ever fails, it is with her. In their false-recognition scene, his riddle-name is *Aithōn,* the "blaze" which melts her (19.204–209) but which she cannot face (19.478). In spite of all the help her disguised husband can give her, she reacts to her dream of the eagle, Odysseus, killing her geese, the suitors, not by preparing for his "return," but by deciding, at last, to give him up for good. After the suitors are dead, and Odysseus has had his bath, she still holds out. Even the appeal to her desire as a woman, effective though it was with Calypso, Nausicaa, and Circe, doesn't work; Odysseus, it appears, will have to sleep alone. In exasperation he asks who moved his bed. In spite of all he has done to make permanent their marriage and the symbol of it, he still cannot tell, he admits, "whether it still stands or whether by now someone has moved it elsewhere, and cut through the trunk of the olive." By this bed and by this exasperation she knows him; flinging her arms around his neck, "Odysseus, don't scold me," she cries, giving him his true name at last. Later, she will accept trouble in more detail. The "immeasurable toil" still to come, none other than the planting of Teiresias' oar, she elects to hear of immediately, though in the first book, after ten years, she could not bear to hear the bard singing of the return from Troy. In the end she takes delight in hearing "all the woes Zeus-sprung Odysseus inflicted on others, and all he himself toiled and suffered." She has accepted the meaning of the name of Odysseus.

Teiresias implied that to win identity one must administer pain, resist all impulses to ignore it, and plant the idea of it in the minds of others. Hence the curious behavior of the hero in making himself known to Laertes. Checking his own tears and resisting the impulse to "kiss his father and embrace him, and tell him all, how he had come and was back at home," Odysseus instead teases the suffering old man with the pain of the loss of his son. This is the pain which killed Anticleia, but it now serves to make clear to Laertes and Odysseus what they mean to each other.

Laertes knows Odysseus by his scar, but also by some fruit trees, given to Odysseus as a boy, which the old man is still tending for him. There is something obviously fruitful in the pain of this relationship between father and son, and the sense of the boar-hunt exploit is there too, especially when later the old man delights to see "son and grandson vying in prowess" in the fight with the suitors' kinsmen. The fruitfulness of trouble has been hinted all along, particularly by the image of the olive. There is the double olive thicket which shelters the hero, naked and alone on Scheria; the green olive stake which puts out Polyphemus' eye; and notably the great olive trunk which makes one corner of Odysseus' bed. The recurrent phrase, *kaka phyteuein* "to plant evils," points to the same fruitfulness. Therefore we can be sure that the life of pain contemplated in the *Odyssey* is fruitful, not sadistic. The ultimate object is recognition and the sense of one's own existence, not the pain itself. The pain necessary to win recognition may be as slight as the show of anger to Penelope, or as great as the blinding of Polyphemus, but in some degree pain will be necessary. Nothing less than the death of 108 suitors (to say nothing of the faithless maids), and the readiness to kill the suitors' kinsmen, will get Odysseus recognized in Ithaca. Once recognition is achieved, however, pain is pointless. At the very end of the poem, Odysseus "swooping like an eagle" on the fleeing ranks of the suitors' adherents, "might have killed them all." Then, "Zeus-sprung son of Laertes, expedient Odysseus, stop!" Athene cries, ". . . lest Zeus be angry at you." The daughter of Zeus herself, as Circe and others have done before her, now hails Odysseus with the rolling epithets of his full titles. Killing beyond the point of this recognition would anger Zeus, would violate the nature of things. But has Zeus not been angry all along at the hero "who received so many buffets, once he had sacked the sacred citadel of Troy?" No. The universe is full of hostility, it includes Poseidon, but it is not ultimately hostile. Zeus has been showing Odysseus not anger, but a terrible fondness, to echo Athene's words quoted early in this paper.

It is thus that the *Odyssey* solves the problem of evil, which it raised at line 62 of the first book. "Excessive suffering," says Zeus, or words to that effect, "is due to folly." "So it is," replies Athene; "but what about Odysseus? Why do you odysseus him so, Zeus?" It is a good question; Zeus admits that Odysseus is the wisest of mankind; yet he permits Poseidon to persecute him. It is a good question, and it contains its own answer. In exposing Odysseus to Poseidon, in allowing him to do and suffer, Zeus is odysseusing Odysseus, giving him his identity. In accepting the implications of his name, Trouble, Odysseus establishes his identity in harmony with the nature of things. In the ultimate sense he is "Zeus-sprung," one whose existence is rooted in life itself.

V

Calypso and Elysium

WILLIAM S. ANDERSON

HOMER, as he did so many other things for Greek culture, established the general outlines of a future happiness, for later poets to elaborate and for religious thinkers to incorporate into the theology of Orphism and of the Eleusinian mysteries. In *Odyssey* 4.561–570 occurs the first extant reference to Elysium, at the point where Menelaus, recounting his experiences in Egypt, cites a special prophecy delivered to him by Proteus, "As for you, divinely nurtured Menelaus, you are not destined to meet your fate and die in horse-raising Argos; but the immortals will send you to the Elysian Plain, to the ends of the earth, where Rhadamanthys of the tawny hair is, where life is supremely easy for men. No hail, no heavy snow, no rain ever falls, but Ocean forever sends over the breezes of the gentle west wind to refresh men. This you will have because you have married Helen and are the son-in-law of Zeus."

I shall not here concern myself with the religious implications of this concept of Elysium, important though they are. Rather, I intend to discuss the meaning of Elysium to Menelaus in the context of the epic and to investigate the structural and semantic relation between Elysium in Book Four and Calypso's Isle in Book Five. Some scholars have questioned this passage and pronounced it a late interpolation because of its religious concepts; other students of Greek religion have defended it as undoubtedly Homeric.[1] But when one considers Proteus' prophecy and its context, it quickly becomes clear that Homer can be more easily defended by literary analysis in this case

Reprinted by permission from *The Classical Journal,* LIV (October, 1958), 2–11. Published by the Classical Association of the Middle West and South, Inc.

than by religious scholarship. Far from being a separable element, the description of a marvelous future existence ultimately depends precisely upon the context in which it is placed, namely, the story told by Menelaus of his arduous voyage back from Troy, the trials he endured for the sake of Zeus' daughter, Helen. I shall accordingly regard *Odyssey* 4.561–570 as genuinely Homeric, because it functions so integrally in the delineation of Menelaus and Sparta.

To see how the Elysian prophecy serves Homer's purpose, it is first necessary to grasp the general tendency of his description of Sparta up to that point. The poet chooses a particular occasion for Telemachus' arrival, for Sparta is celebrating the marriages of Menelaus' two children, Hermione and Megapenthes. This scene of festivity is enhanced by the resplendent appearance of Menelaus' palace. The glitter of the various metals used for ornament and for the banquet instantly provokes the admiration of Telemachus and Peisistratus (4.43 ff.), both of whom come from wealthy homes. Later, Telemachus cannot help exclaiming over all the rich metals on display, and he compares their owner to Zeus himself: the Olympian palace must resemble Menelaus' (4.71 ff.). This first impression, that Menelaus, because we find him on a festal occasion surrounded by striking quantities of wealthy things, must be divinely fortunate, receives immediate qualification from none other than the king himself. Yes, he admits, he is the richest man in the world (80), but he cannot be entirely content with it. Too much has happened as he acquired these splendid things, too much that he can never forget, because he has been directly or indirectly responsible for untold misery. During the seven years that he wandered in the eastern Mediterranean, Agamemnon returned to Argos and was murdered. With that memory, Menelaus can never be satisfied among his possessions (93). In addition, the stage for prosperity was set only by the destruction of his previous home and the loss of countless friends at Troy (95 ff.). In other words, for Menelaus all the glittering precious metals adorning his table and palace inevitably connote the circumstances of the Trojan War: the Rape of Helen which ruined his marriage and made him abandon his palace and people to ten years of neglect, the various friends who fought for his happiness and died, having gained nothing. That past cannot be forgotten, although for a while it may be blotted out by festivity (100 ff.). Finally, Menelaus says that the chief weight on his conscience, the principal blight upon his happiness, springs from his grief for Odysseus, the architect of Greek victory, who alone has not returned home, who has disappeared so that he cannot be called definitely alive or dead (104 ff.).

These opening scenes at Sparta force upon us an ambiguous impression of the king's prosperity, and they very carefully link Menelaus and Odysseus in a relation that remains as yet not entirely clear. While Menelaus luxuriates at home amid an unequalled collection of exotic things from Egypt, Cyprus and North Africa, thoughts come to him of his comrade Odysseus, far away from his home, perhaps dead, certainly the source of grief to the family in Ithaca. It is, we gather at this stage, particularly because of Odysseus that Menelaus' conscience bothers him and refuses him contentment amid his divine wealth. Menelaus contrasts his existence at home with the homelessness of Odysseus, his prosperity with the misery of Odysseus and the family at Ithaca; and that contrast provides us with our first explicit link between the kings of Sparta and Ithaca.

Menelaus has not completely accounted for his discontent, however. If his conscience bothers him over the price paid for the recovery of Helen and the amassment of his wealth, we may legitimately infer that the object of all this effort has not proved so conclusively satisfying as he anticipated, that Helen fails to meet his romantic expectations. Until Helen appears before us, all we know is that Menelaus is dissatisfied, although Homer has shrewdly inserted that detail about the ruined home and allowed Menelaus to express a wish for the days before the Trojan War (97). Now Helen enters, and the poet concentrates on the conditions of their conjugal bliss, with inevitable references to Odysseus again.

Homer immediately compares Helen to the goddess Artemis (122), and the epithet which he applies to Artemis, "the one with the golden distaff," perfectly fits Helen, who also possesses a golden distaff (131). Like the divine Menelaus, his wife enters accompanied with much gold and silver acquired in distant Egypt. In his initial description, then, Homer has emphasized the same qualities in Helen as in Menelaus: divinity, rich surroundings. Now he proceeds to explore the extent of her happiness. Being a woman and more subtle than her husband, Helen never tells us expressly how she feels; on the other hand, we can infer from the way she acts and speaks that her present life is conditioned by past experiences and contentment is not within her reach. She recognizes the resemblance of Telemachus and Odysseus, therefore immediately recalls the Trojan War and her part in it, a very dramatic part indeed. It may seem that she admits her guilt with the epithet of "dog-faced" (145), as though she utterly abominates the woman that she once was. As the scene proceeds, however, Helen shows a distinct affection for those former days and her former self. She weeps with the memory of Troy and its private significance to her, as the others recall their personal involvement in that war (184), as Menelaus relates his plans to settle Odysseus down in one of his Argive cities (174). How fond the memory of Troy is to Helen emerges from her story.

To set the scene properly for Helen's story, Homer relates her use of nepenthe. In Sparta, husband and wife must cast a veil over the past, try to forget the circumstances which brought first Helen, then Menelaus to Troy, merely recall events as adventures which have no bearing upon the present. Oblivion does not come easily, for human feelings go deep and the scars of the past do not disappear. Therefore, to create the ideal conditions for reception of her evocation of the past, Helen must use a drug. Even that drug cannot put to sleep the emotions of Menelaus nor, I suspect, those of Helen. Ostensibly she recounts an adventure of Odysseus which defines his intrepid character, but the heroine of the tale, be it noticed, soon dominates the scene; and that heroine is Helen. We focus our attention on the acute intelligence of this woman who alone recognized the disguised Odysseus, on her secret loyalty to the Greeks, upon her delight in the Trojan grief, and finally upon her changed heart which makes her long for Menelaus and home again. In short, Helen has dramatized herself, recalled her days of glory, and at the same time rather falsified the facts. As the immediate rejoinder of Menelaus in the form of a second Trojan story proves, others interpret her behavior differently. Even after the death of Paris, her longing for her home did not deter her from becoming the lover of Deiphobus (276) nor from unscrupulously misusing the Greeks' desire for their wives in order to lure them, if possible, from the wooden horse. It takes no great effort to imagine the poignancy of Menelaus' memory: his own wife pretending the loving tones of each particular Greek wife, while he crouched there inside the horse, cursing her shamelessness and yet apparently unable to control his own desire for her. Only Odysseus resisted the false Penelope and forced the others to keep quiet.

Two conflicting memories of Troy expose the smouldering emotions that threaten the outward calm of this prosperous scene in Sparta. Menelaus and Helen cannot discuss this past, because each has participated in it in a different, or rather opposing, manner. Menelaus knows that Helen never conclusively broke with the Trojans, never allowed her momentary twinges of shame to disturb for long the pleasant tenor of her life; and Helen knows that she enjoyed the power which she had over history to provoke such a war, could not help but be attracted by the frivolous Paris, could not avoid abusing the uxorious Menelaus. Such recollections cannot be obliterated even by periodic draughts of nepenthe, even by the glittering surroundings of the Spartan palace. The fact is, unlike Penelope, Helen never did anything to remain loyal to Menelaus and never made a convincing effort to return to him. When the husband recovers her, then, he has little to give him satisfaction. If the later legend can be mentioned here, Menelaus may all along have intended to kill Helen for her adultery; but at the crucial moment he proved too weak. In any case, Homer makes evident that possession of Olympian wealth and marriage with Zeus' daughter have not been and are not now able to confer happiness upon Menelaus. Even the festal occasion of the children's marriage becomes qualified with strains of sadness. Hermione, a girl who virtually grew up without a mother, now marries Neoptolemus and embarks upon her tragic experiences of love. Megapenthes' marriage in itself has little significance, but Homer tells us that he is not Helen's son; on this basis, we can immediately interpret the name as an expression of Menelaus' sorrow for his lost wife. With the departure of these two children, if we allow our imagination to wander a little, we can expect that the present tension between husband and wife can only increase. Growing older, with nothing to look forward to in the way of a family or in each other's company, Helen and Menelaus will sit opposite each other, living in their conflicting memories.

The day after Telemachus' arrival at Sparta, Menelaus recounts his wanderings and what he knows of Odysseus. We do not have to go into Menelaus' adventures in Egypt, for they do not add especially to the background which we have already discussed. The seven years of Menelaus' separation from Sparta constitute, of course, the nearest analogy with Odysseus' longer absence; and Homer has continued his subtle contrast. Menelaus roves the eastern Mediterranean, whose associations are prevalently of wealth, drugs, special arts; while Odysseus, we learn, faces alternately monsters and temptations of the flesh in the west. From his experiences, Menelaus learns nothing; he apparently never comes to a reconciliation with his wife except upon the most superficial level, and the only practical result of his travels consists in the wealth which gives him no satisfaction. Odysseus, of course, experiences a considerable change of heart after his many trials. Finally, when he tells of Proteus, Menelaus explicitly associates himself with Odysseus. Immediately before he reports the prediction of his blessed future in Elysium, Menelaus tells what he knows about Odysseus: the Ithacan sits helplessly on the island of Calypso, weeping, without comrades or ship to speed him home over the sea (555–560). With no transition, Proteus then turns to Menelaus and delivers to him the prophecy cited at the beginning of the paper.

On the face of it, the promise of eternal existence would seem quite attractive. The easy existence, the balmy atmosphere, the ideal climate represent a concept of paradise, and, if she were not otherwise qualified, the possession of Helen would seem to epitomize happiness. However, against the background of what Homer has described in Sparta, none of this seems so enticing. Menelaus has surrounded himself with all the physical comforts which wealth can buy, and, although he is in all likelihood the richest man in the world, he has not found happiness in these glittering halls. He has lived with Zeus' daughter for ten years since the destruction of Troy, and still both have little in common and easily yield to their divergent memories of the past. If any man can be said to rival the gods, as Telemachus innocently remarks, Menelaus is that man, with his Olympian wealth and his wife like Artemis. In character, then, Elysium offers him no compensation for earthly trials; rather, it continues the same sensuous tenor of his present existence, continues it indefinitely. Since Menelaus cannot relax in the comforts of Sparta, where at least he can expect some alterations of climate, it seems hard to accept his Elysian future as an unqualified good. As I have already argued, Menelaus' future is inevitably conditioned by his past;

and, as I have intimated and now shall suggest, it is also strongly modified by the contrasting values of Odysseus.

Telemachus' visit to Sparta occupies most of Book Four, but in the last 220 lines Homer shifts the scene back to Ithaca, to re-emphasize the desperate condition of Penelope and her son, to reassert the need for Odysseus, and finally to make patent the sharp difference between Sparta and Ithaca. At Sparta, the comfortable environment barely conceals the tensions between husband and wife. At Ithaca, the dangers and temptations surrounding Penelope serve to define her unchanging devotion to her husband. One element is missing from the contrast, though repeatedly alluded to in Book Four, and Homer supplies it in the beginning of Book Five. On Calypso's Isle, the poet presents Odysseus overcoming temptations which define his attitude not only towards home, but, even more important, towards life itself.[2] The significance of the hero's action becomes especially clear, I hope to show, because Homer has carefully placed Odysseus in the very environment which has been promised to Menelaus.

The reasons which lead me to compare Elysium and Calypso's Isle of Ogygia may be summarized under the following five headings: (1) both Elysium and Ogygia are imaginary places; (2) both are islands; (3) both are located far to the west, presumably in the Atlantic; (4) both enjoy similar climate and ease of life; (5) both possess important associations with death. For the purposes of deriving the significance of this comparison, the last two reasons have special importance, and I shall expand upon them. The first three can be treated rather briefly, with the detail relegated to notes.

The very concept of Elysium makes it imaginary, for it defies the very essence of the real world: a physical limit on existence. Most scholars consider Ogygia imaginary, too,[3] and those, like Bérard,[4] who have searched for it have failed to convince others. Again and again, we hear that Ogygia is an island. Homer's description of Elysium allows several interpretations, but, located *at* the limits of the earth, it certainly can suggest an island in Ocean *beyond* the limits of the earth. Within a short time after Homer wrote, at any rate, the concept of Elysium and that of the Isle or Isles of the Blessed became inextricably fused, as Hesiod illustrates.[5] By the fifth century, Euripides can permit the Dioscuroi to predict to Menelaus that he will escape death and go to the Isles of the Blest.[6] As for the geographical location of these imaginary islands, Homer's details and ancient tradition have set them far in the west, though not universally in the Atlantic. Elysium lies at the limits of the earth in Ocean, and, since the Greeks could only have known in Homer's time of the continental limits and existence of the ocean in the west (having explored the eastern Mediterranean), Homer's brief description suggests the west. Later writers unanimously placed Elysium's equivalent, the Isles of the Blessed, farther and farther away in the Atlantic,[7] and we actually hear of Sertorius' project of sailing thither to escape his enemies.[8] Ogygia was variously placed by poets and geographers from near Crete to points on the southern coast of Italy to the Atlantic Ocean.[9] On the basis of what Homer says, the Atlantic location so strenuously urged by Strabo [10] seems more than likely. Clearly, from the sailing directions of Odysseus' raft and the time necessary to reach Phaeacia, the island lies far in the west.[11] Furthermore, an argument which has not been used before, visibility in the Mediterranean is such that Odysseus would have been able to see some other land from any point on a clear day; which Homer expressly denies to his hero.[12] All in all, Elysium and Ogygia tally remarkably well as islands situated in approximately the same general environment.

The climates of the two islands assume considerable importance in Homer's description, for they bear directly upon the significance of the places to their residents, Menelaus or Odysseus. The balmy wind, the freedom from seasonal variation, in contrast of course with the climate which the Greeks experienced, convey the data necessary to support Homer's assertion, that life in Elysium is supremely easy. Such a life, as the fact that Menelaus has earned it through marriage with Zeus' daughter suggests, approximates divine felicity. The same freedom from seasonal changes Homer attributes to the gods' residence (6.43 ff.). Ogygia, too, proves so congenial to divine senses that, on his arrival there, Hermes pauses in admiration (5.73–74). The scene which has evoked Hermes' admiration possesses all the qualities of the island paradise: Ogygia has luxuriant growth of trees and vines, swarms with birds, abounds in water; and colorful flowers dot nearby meadows. All centers on the cave of Calypso, from which emerge the seductive notes of the nymph's song and the pleasant scent of burning cedar logs (5.58 ff.). This idyllic description implies the same gentle regularity of climate as on Elysium, the same effortlessness of existence. Like Elysium, therefore, Ogygia can confer upon Odysseus immortality, with all that the term connotes of security and sensuous ease. But, just as Menelaus earns his immortality through Helen, so Odysseus can become deathless only by succumbing forever to the divine Calypso.

Finally, both Elysium and Ogygia possess important associations with death. According to the prophecy of Proteus, Menelaus will escape death in Argos and be transported to the felicity of Elysium, from which we can infer that Elysium represents the desire for and possibility of personal survival after death. Because of his connection with the semi-divine Helen, Menelaus himself attains a divine state of existence, escaping the fate allotted to humanity as a whole. We have already discussed the impression which such felicity makes against the background of Sparta. In the case of Calypso's Isle, the immortality offered to Odysseus contains many suggestions not of eternal life, but of eternal death. The funereal overtones of Ogygia have been carefully studied in Hermann Güntert's *Kalypso,* a book which frequently connects Ogygia and Elysium, as, for instance, in the following sentence: "Die ideal gezeichnete, friedliche Landschaft, die Hermes zum Verweilen einlädt, sie schildert also nichts anderes als Auen eines Elysions, als die Gärten eines westlichen, weltfernen Toteneilands." [13] ["The ideally sketched and tranquil landscape, which invites Hermes to tarry, depicts then nothing other than the meadow of an Elysium, the gardens of a western, other-worldly Island of Death."] Güntert takes the traditional etymology of Calypso's name, the "Concealer," and, because of Homer's usage of the verb *kalúptein,* specifically interprets Calypso as "she who buries."[14] He interprets the name Ogygia as referring to the Underworld, Stygian.[15] The trees and flowers surrounding the cave of the nymph, conceivable as an entrance to Hades, connote death.[16] The black alder (*klé·thre·*) is probably funereal; the black poplar (*aígeiros*) Homer describes as growing also in Hades, in the glades of Persephone;[17] and the cypress still marks the location of cemeteries in Italy and Greece. The flowery meadows, parallel to the fields of asphodel through which Achilles strides (11.539), display parsley and the purple iris, both associated with the funeral ritual.[18] Finally, in all western folklore and poetry, as Güntert observes, Love and Death unite in a semantic complex of the greatest importance in interpreting human relations and motivations.[19] The pre-Wagnerian theme of Tannhäuser and Frau Venus shows a remarkable resemblance to that of Odysseus and Calypso. One can forget oneself in love, one can actually and symbolically die in love, as Shakespeare so carefully depicts Antony doing. Calypso then, in one sense, is death, with all its attractions of escape and self-indulgence.

I conclude that Homer has described Ogygia in this particular way, to make clear what Odysseus abandons: he has at his disposal all that Menelaus someday will receive, and he rejects it. Such a contrast, implicit in the juxtaposition of Odysseus and Menelaus, Ogygia and Elysium, in Proteus' speech, becomes increasingly pronounced, and therefore more significant, as a reult of the detailed similarity between the two islands. Menelaus will end his human life by escaping to Elysium, where he will enjoy permanent ease in an atmosphere worthy of the son-in-law of Zeus; Odysseus begins his human life again by escaping from that oblivious ease offered him by Calypso, the one who buries.

We have seen how Menelaus' past inevitably qualifies his future on Elysium, making it seem far less delightful than its superficial characteristics would suggest. In the same way, the events leading up to Odysseus' arrival on Ogygia help to interpret the threat of Calypso. However, Homer's organization of his story stresses the most important aspect of Odysseus' adventures, especially by the close relation between Elysium and Ogygia: namely, that decisive act of leaving Calypso. Thus, just as our last impression of Menelaus suggests his end, so our first impression of Odysseus signifies the beginning of his return, therefore of life itself. To see the departure in its complete perspective, we have to refer to the autobiographical account of Books Nine through Twelve, in which the hero explains how he came to be driven up alone on Calypso's isle.[20]

The adventures of Odysseus after leaving Troy alternate between various types of violence and varieties of sensual temptations, the first receiving its greatest emphasis in the encounter with Polyphemus, the second in the meeting with Circe. In all cases, Odysseus proves superior to his men, but not entirely exempt from the harmful effects of these experiences. After conquering Circe, he lets himself to a certain extent be conquered in turn and remains idly with her for a year until his men protest. Even with the forewarning of

Circe, he insists on experiencing the song of the Sirens (against which he can offer no resistance) and attempting to appeal to his own futile strength to repel Scylla. It is indeed a helpless leader who sleeps while his men are committing the sacrilege, eating the cattle of the Sun, about which Teiresias has warned him. From the shipwreck which immediately engulfs his men, which provides a clear comment on Odysseus' failure as leader of men, only the hero escapes and after ten days of drifting is cast up on Calypso's isle. Briefly summarized, this is the tale that Odysseus tells Alcinous, and the hero makes no pretense of priding himself on his achievements. As he says in the form of an introduction, he has suffered considerably (9.15) and the process of homecoming has inflicted many sorrows upon him (9.37). The architect of victory at Troy, who is washed up on Ogygia with no men to enhance his prestige, with no splendid clothes and weapons or any of the other loot of Troy or Ismarus, bruised and battered by ten days of exposure to the salt and sun, this man is symbolically stripped of all his heroic veneer and must face his new adventures with only the resources of his own dubious character.

Homer tells us nothing of that long period of seven years, approximately equal to the term of Menelaus' voyages, which Odysseus spent on Ogygia, or almost nothing. At an early stage, Calypso must have made that attractive offer of immortality. She had saved him from the sea and nursed him, brought him back to health (5.130 ff.), and she had loved him. Nor was the love only on one side. When Homer finally, after the preparation of Books One through Four, gives us our first picture of the actual Odysseus, he describes the hero weeping and immediately offers therefor two interrelated explanations: Odysseus longs for his home, for the nymph *no longer* pleases him (5.152–153). That little word *oukéti* conveys a world of meaning. We see Odysseus at the crucial moment; behind that lie seven years which have apparently only gradually produced this decisive state of mind. Now, he goes to bed with the beauteous Calypso under compulsion, "cold lover with an ardent dame," as Rieu translates 5.155; but we would not be wrong in assuming that the habit implies an original mutual ardency. However, Homer allows us to set an earlier limit on his hero's oblivious enjoyment, for Proteus, nearly three years before this time, had envisioned Odysseus on Ogygia already weeping for home, already detained against his will (4.555 ff.). The interval between then and now has been spent in confirming that will of Odysseus, in hardening his purpose to make unswervingly for Ithaca; he is not to leave Calypso only to fall under the spell of another woman. All he wants, as we learn in Book One, is to see the smoke of his own hearth and know that he has come home (57–59).

The seven years of this sojourn with Calypso, in the economy of the epic, render this the most severe trial of the hero. With no external commitments, with none of his martial and kingly accouterments to remind him of his position, Odysseus must search his own conscience and find his purpose in life. It is for this reason that I urge the parallelism between Elysium and Ogygia, especially the themes of entire physical comfort and the escape from life which immortality confers. The hero has reached a stage which others, including Menelaus, regard as the supreme goal of existence. Even Odysseus, after his futile efforts against Poseidon and his long struggle with the incorrigible natures of his men, found such a paradise to his liking, for a while. No men came to him after a year, as they had on Circe's island, to remind him of his responsibility. He could relax and pretend that all he really desired after the ten years of war at Troy was an eternity of ease with a beautiful woman, rather a divine nymph, at his disposal. So he did relax. He could of course rationalize his behavior to himself by saying that he was helpless, he had no ship, no means of leaving Ogygia. Therefore, he was helpless. From the perspective of the living, he had become dead. The suitors in Ithaca were vying for his wife on the assumption that he would never return. Telemachus had lost all hope in the father who was but a name to him. Only Penelope remained faithful to a living Odysseus, yet with much hesitation and soul-searching. At the end of Book Four Penelope weeps not only for her lion-hearted husband but also for Telemachus, who is threatened with the suitors' ambush. When both husband and wife weep with longing for each other, when Penelope fears her husband's death and Odysseus bewails his loss of life's values, then the stage for reunion has been set.

Güntert's emphasis on Calypso as a goddess of death presiding over an Elysian island must also be given its poetic interpretation. Besides the fact stated above, that the hero had become dead to his family and friends, we should see what Calypso means to Odysseus himself. On Ogygia, as Menelaus will some day in Elysium, Odysseus had escaped from all the practical problems of life. In an atmosphere that appealed entirely to his senses and merely demanded his compliance, he sank into oblivion, forgotten and forgetting. All that life had signified before this, the constant struggle against the sea, the shrewd persistence at Troy, the original dedication to Ithaca and his family, ceaseless activity with an intelligent goal in sight, all this was entirely negated by Calypso. She required moral abandonment. Without pressing the psychological term, we can perhaps think of Odysseus as yielding for a while to his "death-wish," especially after all the trials that he had been through with his men. Just as he experienced one form of death in the visit to the shades, so now he experiences another form of death, this time his own, in a protracted period of sensual abandonment. Calypso buries him in her island paradise, until he reasserts his former will. When we see him for the first time, he has conquered death; despite all the attractions of the island and its nymph, he has turned his back on it all, fastened his gaze on the horizon, and his thoughts now negate Calypso with their sharp focus on Ithaca.[21] Odysseus is alive again. Therefore the gods act to set him free of his prison of death.

Throughout the first four books Homer has been preparing us for our first sight of Odysseus, by describing the character and value of the man as seen through others' eyes. He has carefully contrasted the serenity of Pylos and the comforts of Sparta with the plundered, riotous palace in Ithaca. It should not surprise us, therefore, if the scene at Sparta also serves to sharpen the outlines of the portrait of Odysseus. Proteus' speech juxtaposes the weeping Odysseus on Ogygia with the presumably contented Menelaus in Elysium. Similarly, when we actually confront Homer's hero, the memory of life in Sparta and its projection in Elysium remain. In short, the poet has added perspective by which we can judge the character of Odysseus, a man who starts from the limits of Menelaus' character; and we therefore should find the transition to Book Five relatively easy. In this respect, Page has made an interesting suggestion in his recent book on the *Odyssey*.[22] Admiring the artistic movement from Telemachus to Penelope to Odysseus, offended by the repetitious beginning of Book Five, with what seems a senseless assembly of the gods, Page argues that the Assembly represents a later interpolation of the Homeridae, who, singing a portion of Homer's epic beginning with the hero's appearance, needed some sort of introduction to the events and the hero. If true, the original juxtaposition of the scene on Ogygia to those in Ithaca and Sparta would stress even more forcefully the contrast between the hero and Menelaus. While Menelaus looks bitterly to the past or wearily to his Elysian escape from life, Odysseus emerges from the past a new man, entirely committed to living values. His greatness depends utterly on his humanity, his mortality. The Greeks understood clearly Odysseus' rejection of Calypso, and tradition has respected him by never assigning him to Elysium.[23]

VI

The Obstacles to Odysseus' Return

CHARLES H. TAYLOR, JR.

THE VITALITY OF Odysseus' adventures during his travels home has always fascinated readers of the *Odyssey*. Their extraordinary diversity is generally thought today to derive from the collection in Books Five through Twelve of motifs from a wide range of folk tales. However, a variety of sources for Odysseus' adventures does not prove an absence of unity among them. On the contrary, their artistic unity has been felt so strongly by some critics that they have developed elaborate arguments showing that these adventures form a logical progression in the moral and social education of the hero. Only after learning from them, they claim, is Odysseus fit to return to Ithaca. Such arguments are often enlightening in their interpretation of individual episodes, and Odysseus does gain from some of his adventures experience which is valuable to him later. Nevertheless, Odysseus is basically, as Cedric Whitman puts it, "a fixed personality," equipped from the beginning to manage almost any situation in which he finds himself.[1] Unlike Achilles, Odysseus experiences no division of the will.

Yet we remain confronted with the feeling that these marvelous encounters, so many of them imbued with magic or the supernatural, have a consistent bearing on the hero's role in the poem. Instead of depicting primarily his progressive development, they reveal the nature of his already developed character. They enable us to understand why he is able to achieve what he does and what the meaning of that achievement is. Although the source of the hero's accomplish-

Reprinted by permission from *The Yale Review*, L (Summer, 1961) 569–580. I have added notes and made a few changes in the text.

ment is rather his maturity than his growth, his struggles are with the enemies of growth.

Odysseus' goal throughout his adventures is his destined return to Ithaca. W. B. Stanford, adopting Joyce's term, distinguishes Homer's Odysseus as a "centripetal" hero, in contrast to many of his followers in the Ulyssian tradition.[2] His basic urge, Stanford reminds us, is not to explore, but to make his way home.

It has been pointed out frequently that this desire to return is motivated by the Homeric hero's characteristic devotion to fame and reputation. Odysseus would always be honored for having been the cleverest of the Greeks at Troy, but only when he regains his place as King of Ithaca can he complete his fame as the most resourceful of men, equal to any challenge.[3]

Intent on his reputation, Odysseus is naturally concerned with his name. In the Cyclops episode, his pride in his name leads him to taunt the monster with the identity of his conqueror, thereby enabling Polyphemus to call upon him the savage wrath of Poseidon. From this rash act, Odysseus learns that it is sometimes essential to keep his name to himself, as we see him do later both in his anonymous approach to the Phaeacians and in the disciplined maintenance of his disguise upon his arrival in Ithaca. But these disguises are only temporary sacrifices of his identity for the present in the interest of establishing it beyond compare for the future. Rash or cautious, Odysseus' dedication to his reputation always reflects his care for his identity.

Many of the extraordinary obstacles to Odysseus' return are in the form of temptations. Yet they are not so much temptations to sexual immorality or social irresponsibility as they are temptations to the surrender of his individuality. The encounter with the Lotus-eaters epitomizes many of the temptations which follow. Feeding on the lotus makes Odysseus' men νόστου λαθέσθαι (9.97), "forget their homeward journey." They desire instead to live like vegetarian animals and resist being brought back to the world of human hardships and responsibilities. The eater of the lotus becomes like an infant who is well-fed and contented, for the environment supports him without demanding anything in return. The lotus-eater loses all consciousness of self, of being an individual with origins of his own. For a man of Odysseus' powerful intelligence this is an easy temptation to resist, easier than some of those which follow. He quickly recognizes that eating the lotus is self-destructive, for he tells the Phaeacians that it was not literal death which the Lotus-eaters planned for his men, but the narcotic effects of the lotus instead. That this holds no attraction for Odysseus underscores an important dimension of his heroic character. He is always conscious of who he is and of what he wants to achieve and is never willing to trade this consciousness for some kind of euphoria.

The most obvious menace to Odysseus' identity during his travels is death by water. To drown at sea, Poseidon's constant threat, is to vanish utterly from the world of men. This is a fate far worse than death in battle, a proper end to a heroic career. More than once Odysseus wishes he had fallen at Troy, for thus at least he could have bequeathed his son a famous name. Facing instead what seems a hopeless struggle against Poseidon's awful power, he must resist many times the temptation to allow himself to die. Once, the temptation is explicit, when he debates whether he should drown himself after his companions have let the winds out of the bag, while on other occasions the temptation is implied in his expressions of dismay when he thinks he has been saved to no avail. His profound disappointment makes his knees quake when after swimming for two days and two nights he finds himself off the isle of Scheria only to discover that reefs and cliffs make the shore unapproachable. By this time, however, he has learned from Achilles in Hades that life, wretched as it may be, is always preferable to death. So, despite his misery and exhaustion, he weighs the alternatives with careful discrimination, trying to decide whether to attempt a risky landing or to expose himself again to the open ocean. He refuses to relax his intelligence and permit himself to disappear in the unknown depths of the engulfing sea.

In many of Odysseus' other adventures, the temptation to surrender his individual identity is perhaps less obvious, but no less real. Beautiful and soft, Calypso carries the appeal of the eternal feminine. She offers Odysseus much more than the lotus can: not only an escape from physical suffering, but lovely sexuality and eternal life as well. Not only will the environment nurture him like an infant in the womb—note the image of Calypso's cave—but, unlike the infant, he will retain his identity as a male and be able to share the pleasures of sexual differentiation with the goddess. But this is all he will retain of his identity, for with Calypso he can no longer be Odysseus the hero. If he accepts Calypso's offer, he will be no more than the consort of a minor goddess. Impervious to death he will remain, to be sure, but for that very reason he will be unable to run any of the risks which make survival a heroic achievement. Instead, he would have to surrender himself to the instinctual female principle, physically vital, but intellectually and spiritually lifeless. Odysseus' surrender to Calypso would involve the loss both of his outward identity as πολύτλας Odysseus, the man who suffers and endures, and of his inner identity as a separate individual free to come to terms with life on his own. He would have no self, but would exist only as an appendage to the goddess, serving her desire.

Odysseus refuses Calypso's offer of bodily immortality for the same reasons that he resists bodily death: in neither case could he preserve his whole being as Odysseus. Fleshly immortality with Calypso is no more complete than the fleshless immortality so forcefully disparaged by Achilles.

Calypso, Athene tells Zeus at the beginning of the poem, is trying to make Odysseus forget Ithaca; the analogy with the temptation of the Lotus-eaters is clear enough. What is perhaps less clear is that Circe's charms are directed to the same end. She drugs Odysseus' men, not at once to turn them to swine, but ἵνα πάγχυ λαθοίατο πατρίδος αἴης (10.236), "that they might quite forget their native land." Only after the drug takes effect does she strike them with her rod and pen them in her sties. The sequence of events is significant because it presents the metamorphosis as a corollary of forgetting one's native land. The transformation of man to animal is a vivid image of the lessening of human consciousness which forgetting one's origins implies. Men who let themselves be drugged into a lower level of awareness by the destructive power of the enchantress, the story suggests, become no more than animals to be kept as the woman's pets.

But for Odysseus the consequences of encountering Circe are very different. Homer says that Hermes gave Odysseus the herb moly as an antidote to the enchantress' potion. Yet who has a better claim to divine aid than Odysseus? Possessing more intelligence and will-power than other men, he is ideally equipped to resist the hypnotic powers of Circe's enchantment. She herself never complains that Odysseus has been aided by a god; rather, her response to Odysseus' refusal to succumb to her potion is that he is a man whose mind is proof against enchantment. Unable to subdue him, with characteristic womanly duality she desires to surrender herself instead, imploring him to come to her bed. He, in turn, is obligated to accept her offer, once he is assured he can do so on his own terms. To avoid submission to Circe's destructive power does not mean that her positive feminine values need be rejected. On the contrary, Odysseus' heroic individuality is partly defined by his capacity to encounter the essence of the female principle without being overwhelmed by it.

Circe, then, embodies both the destructive and the creative aspects of the feminine, and Odysseus profits from the latter. It is scarcely surprising that he finds her exotic knowledge and complex sexuality more interesting than Calypso's immortal ease. He enjoys her company so much that even after a year he has to be prodded by his men into continuing on his way.

Though Odysseus temporarily loses his sense of urgency with Circe, there is never any question whether he intends ultimately to resume his journey. There is, indeed, only one occasion when he consciously wishes to yield to a temptation, even though he knows it would mean his destruction. Despite Circe's explicit warning of the mortal danger, he wishes to stop and hear the Sirens' song. Since he takes the precautions Circe has advised, he is unable to yield, but it is revealing that this one time he wishes he could.

The unique appeal of the Sirens emphasizes once again Odysseus' concern for his personal identity. Besides embodying the seductive attractions of feminine allure and poetic song, the Sirens' words are especially calculated to make Odysseus wish to yield. They appeal to him in terms of their knowledge of his renown as "great glory of the Achaeans," their appreciation of the heroes' suffering at Troy, and their understanding of events to come. Thus it seems to Odysseus that his conscious desire for identity, reputation, and knowledge is at one with his masculine urge to enjoy the feminine. The irony is that this illusory union of his higher and lower desires will mean in fact the loss of his life and thus of the heroic identity for which he cares so much. The apparent wholeness of the Sirens' appeal makes it an irresistible temptation and temporarily causes Odysseus to lose control of his will.

But in the final trial before his return to Ithaca, Odysseus is magnificently aware of his true objectives. Though he is never personally moved by the possibility of marrying Nausicaa, he is careful not to preclude it as a possibility. Only after he has been guaranteed passage home and everything is prepared for his departure, does he reveal who he is. His opening address to Nausicaa when she comes upon him by the shore is a supremely subtle invitation to consider him as a potential husband, yet it does not commit him as an acknowledged suitor. Although she is not a goddess and cannot make him immortal, in one way Nausicaa is more attractive than Calypso. Because she is mortal, with her Odysseus could take his place in a world in which heroic action is possible. Still, the utopian setting of Phaeacian life tends to vitiate the need for heroism. Once again the temptation is to escape from the struggle for survival which requires such alertness. With Nausicaa, Odysseus would not have to be subordinate to a woman (unless we feel that Arete's domination of Alcinous implies this possibility) but he would have to accept, without earning it, the unheroic relaxation which music, feasting, clean linen, and gregarious sociability encourage. Moreover, whatever reputation he might achieve in Scheria could never be of a piece with his fame as Odysseus the inventor of the Trojan Horse and Lord of the Ithacans. As Odysseus, he would not be eligible for Nausicaa's hand, having already a wife and obligations of his own. Concerned with his identity, he naturally prefers to return, even to the enormous challenges which he knows will face him in Ithaca.

Thus it is clear that whether Odysseus faces a temptation or a threat, an opportunity to evade suffering or a danger of being crushed by it, the challenge is always to his survival as Odysseus. The essentially equivalent menace of the temptation to ease, on the one hand, and of the threat to life, on the other, is nicely suggested in the encounter with the Laestrygonians. There, Odysseus' ship alone survives because he refuses to be tempted by the smooth waters of the protected harbor. To seek the easier resting place is to invite destruction. By lying outside, although exposed to the discomforts of poorer protection from the weather, he is able to cut his cables and flee when the frightful attack of the man-eating Laestrygonians begins. Because he is willing to accept more suffering than other men, Odysseus avoids being swallowed up by the monstrous giants.

Despite the variety of situations which they present, then, Odysseus' adventures during his homeward journey repeatedly confront him with some kind of threat to his identity as hero. But they have more in common than that, for nearly every threat also manifests the forces at work in man's natural environment. Whether Odysseus is endangered by predatory monsters, narcotic herbs, feminine sexuality, or the violence of the sea, he experiences in each case the realm of nature and instinct. The strength of his opponents is rooted either in the external natural world or in the non-rational elements within human nature.

Poseidon, Odysseus' greatest enemy, is only superficially detached from the natural environment by his designation as an Olympian deity. Of all the Olympians, he is the most immersed in the elements. Although he attends gatherings on Olympus, his sphere of action is the Mediterranean waters and his home is deep in the Aegean Sea. Three of his epithets tie him directly to the earth, for he is γαιήοχος, "earth-holder," and ἐνοσίχθων or ἐννοσίγαιος, "earth-shaker." Moreover, the most satisfactory explanation of his name is that he was once πόσις Δᾶς, spouse of Da or Demeter, the earth goddess.[4] The evidence now strongly suggests that he was chthonic in his origins, and it is therefore the less surprising that as he actually functions in the *Odyssey* he is still so—the god of a violent sea.

It has been said that the Homeric poems are remarkably free of the chthonic cults and powers which were widespread in contemporary popular culture. Of chthonic cults this is certainly true; in the *Odyssey,* even the earthbound deities Calypso and Circe are carefully subordinated to the Olympian system, as Hermes' errands show. Poseidon, as we have noted, is theologically an important part of the system, and the monstrous Polyphemus is given an Olympian heritage. But like Poseidon, Calypso in her cave and Circe keeping men as domesticated animals are indeed chthonic personalities.

Homer's recognition of the influence of these earthbound divinities never takes the form of ritual devotions, but it is respectful nevertheless. Odysseus must demonstrate his ability to withstand their powers, whether seductive or destructive, without scorning them. It is partly his contempt for Polyphemus which brings him so much pain at the hand of Poseidon. He suffers for foolishly supposing that a monster might behave like a civilized host and for taunting the brute whom he has duped. Only after he has lived out the consequences of this disdain and come to terms with many representatives of instinct and violence can he achieve his return.

It is noteworthy that in all Odysseus' adventures in Books Nine through Twelve, excepting the single intercession of Hermes on Aeaea, Odysseus receives no Olympian aid. His opponents, for all their nominal subjection to Olympian authority, are left to exercise their powers unopposed by champions of Olympian values. Indeed, Odysseus receives more aid from Circe, following his conquest of her, and from the inhabitants of the underworld to which she directs him, than he does from anything but his own wits and determination. Thus we can say that chthonian powers are not so much absent from the *Odyssey* as they are subdued or brought into his service by the hero's extraordinary feats of will and intelligence.

The Olympian whose neglect of Odysseus during his travels is most conspicuous is Athene. When she reveals herself to him after he has been put ashore on Ithaca, Odysseus pointedly reminds her that she had showed him no favor during the years between his departure from Troy and his arrival at the land of the Phaeacians. Prior to leaving Ogygia, he had to manage without her aid. Yet when the poem opens, it is she who is urging Zeus to free him from Calypso so that he can pursue his homeward journey. He has assumed for her by this time a very personal value and she interests herself in all his subsequent adventures.

In their spirited conversation in Book Thirteen, Athene tells Odysseus that she reveres him because he is, in Rieu's words, "so civilized, so intelligent, so self-possessed" (ἐπητής ἀγχίνοος, and ἐχέφρων 13.332).[5] These are the qualities which distinguish Odysseus from other men, including other heroes; they are the hallmarks of his identity. We see his intelligent self-possession again and again as he parries the threats and blandishments of his opponents. It is for this keen-witted firmness of mind that Athene becomes devoted to him.

Like Odysseus, Athene is intelligent, cunning, and strong-willed, possessing as a goddess the attributes which enable the hero to survive. When she comes to his assistance, she reinforces his strengths, but only after he has proven himself capable of survival without her aid. Rather than acting as the effective cause of his success, she stands instead as a symbol or projection of that already within Odysseus which makes him successful.

Hesiod tells us that Athene sprang full-grown from the head of Zeus. Conceived the daughter of Metis, her associations with wise counsel and the values of the head are as evident in her origins as in her adoption of Odysseus. She represents that intelligent awareness which characterizes the hero.

Probing the meaning of their alliance more deeply, we find Athene, Odysseus' genuinely Olympian advocate, in direct opposition to Poseidon and the other essentially earthbound powers. Just as she emblems Odysseus' rational consciousness, the chthonic forces she opposes symbolize the non-rational core of man's nature. Projected as external threats and temptations, they image in reality the powers which menace the identity of the hero from beneath the surface of consciousness.

The analogy between these external forces and the biological foundations of human nature is suggested in the poem through the dangers of sleep. In the debacle with the bag of winds, Odysseus fails to reach Ithaca because sleep overcomes him. Though the body lives, the saving consciousness which defines the hero departs. It was "cruel sleep" (10.68–69), Odysseus tells Aeolus, which was his undoing. Later, he is "in pitiless sleep" (12.372) when his comrades slaughter the Oxen of the Sun. Odysseus cannot be held responsible for the failure of his men on this occasion, for he has warned them fully. Nevertheless, it is while he sleeps that the catastrophe occurs. Similarly, the youthful Elpenor loses his life because he has neither the will-power nor the intelligence to dispel the fogginess induced by wine and sleep. Unlike Odysseus, he is not proof against enchantment.

It is remarkable, too, how many of the specific threats to Odysseus suggest symbolically the magnetic attraction of the unconscious in the human psyche. The sea is an ancient emblem of the whole realm of the irrational, and drowning in the sea a compelling image of being overwhelmed from below, returning to the elemental. In the picture of Odysseus clinging doggedly to the fig tree above Charybdis' whirlpool we find a striking representation of the struggle between conscious determination and the downward pull of subterranean forces. Calypso's womblike cave and Circe's pet swine depict the appeals of returning to infancy or animality where one lives unaware of personal selfhood. Like Calypso, Polyphemus is an earthbound cave-dweller. As the son of Poseidon he is allied with the natural violence of the sea. Moreover, his identifying feature is his single eye, an arresting image of half-consciousness. With his primitive vision, he is naturally both hostile and vulnerable to Odysseus' civilized intelligence.

Thus it seems to me that Odysseus' struggles for survival and identity convey more than the recognized Homeric values of fame and reputation as their ends. To apply the metaphor both more personally and more broadly, part of the poem's appeal rests in the way it suggests the struggle for individual consciousness against the forces for primitive absorption in the instinctual world. This is a fundamental meaning of nearly every hero story. It is a struggle every human being experiences as he strives to achieve a degree of genuine individuality and self-awareness. In Odysseus, the struggle displays a fixed personality more than a growing one because, unlike most men, he almost always wins. This does not mean that for Odysseus the struggle is easy; rather, we are fully aware of the mortal threat in each encounter and repeatedly impressed with the quality of character which enables Odysseus to conquer it. Odysseus' success makes him not less human but more completely human, the example of a man enabled by his maturity to cope with multifarious challenges to his accomplished selfhood.

Telemachus' gradual discovery of the meaning of his identity as his father's son, on the other hand, shows the normal growth of the youthful personality. As he puts away the childishness of helpless daydreaming about his father's return, he becomes equipped by his own sea-journey to help Odysseus meet the greatest challenge of his heroic career. With determined cunning, they effect together the destruction of the suitors. The poet emphasizes Telemachus' developing maturity by having him displace his mother as head of the household in his father's absence. While Telemachus outgrows subjection to the personal mother, Odysseus refuses to submit to the elemental forces of the whole domain of nature.

Bruno Snell insists that the abstractions which deal with the nature of the self are not present in Homer's vocabulary.[6] But to note that it was not possible for Homer to discuss such problems abstractly does not mean that therefore they are not problems for him at all. It is widely acknowledged that one of Homer's ways of representing inner events, particularly those caused by non-rational impulses, is to project them by means of the divine machinery in his poems. My point is that the extraordinary encounters of Odysseus in his travels function in much the same manner.

E. R. Dodds shows that Homeric man believed what was not rational in his behavior was not really a part of himself, and the resulting projection of the irrational upon external powers produced a culture in which shame, not guilt, was dominant. The shift from shame-culture to guilt-culture in the centuries between Homer and Aeschylus he ascribes partly to progressive recognition that most of the evil men do, whether consciously determined or not, is actually generated from within themselves.

Increasing consciousness does bring with it increased moral awareness, and, often, a sense of sin. Yet, as I see it, another reason there is more guilt-consciousness in the later writers is that they have more to feel guilty about. Dodds himself conjectures that their sense of guilt is somehow related to the extremely patriarchal society which had by then evolved. Besides attributing the sense of guilt to repressed feelings of hostility toward the father-order, as Dodds does, I would assign it primarily to unconscious recognition that the earthbound and all it stands for have been undervalued. The powerful feelings of guilt are derived ultimately from undue disregard of the claims of the non-rational. An additional tension would be caused by rebellion against the consciously accepted patriarchy, but the Aeschylean "haunted, oppressive atmosphere" of which Dodds speaks[7] springs essentially from the vengeance in the unconscious of the matriarchal Furies.

There is none of this atmosphere in the *Odyssey*. Although Odysseus, as we have seen, stands for the values of consciousness, there is not yet that contempt for the feminine and the irrational which brings with it a sense of guilt. This will come later because the trend of conscious development is patriarchal and is accompanied after a time by reduced esteem for the female. Erich Neumann observes that since the unconscious is generally given a feminine character, the depreciation of the unconscious in cultural development becomes confused with a belittling of feminine values.[8] In the *Odyssey,* however, there is no such confusion. The characterizations of Helen, of Arete, of Nausicaa, and of Penelope, not to mention Athene, show each to be worthy of respect and admiration. Odysseus (or Telemachus) honors each appropriately and there is no hint that each, in her own way, is not at least the equal of her masculine opposite. Odysseus accepts the favors of Calypso and of Circe, even as he refuses to surrender his will to them. Although Poseidon is masculine, we have noted that he is closely related to the chthonic feminine. He too must be respected, as we see both in the dire consequences of wounding his son and in Teiresias' insistence upon Odysseus' duty to carry his homage to a people who think an oar a "winnowing fan."

Odysseus' quest for identity is in fact profoundly involved with the feminine. In seeking the wholeness of his being, he passes through intimate experience with various embodiments of archetypal woman, each reflecting some aspect of what he as masculine hero lacks. The majority of these women pose the temptation of a return to the matriarchal order, where a man may be killed or be comfortable, but is dead as a hero in either case. Athene's femininity alone is not earthbound and instinctual, for she is associated instead with those intellectual and spiritual values which distinguish civilized human beings. In their purest form these qualities are mysterious and reside as much above normal consciousness as the instinctual do below it. Thus they too have a feminine coloring and are frequently represented by women in the metaphors of art.

But for Odysseus throughout his journey, Penelope is the woman he seeks. For all her beauty, Athene's Olympian dignity offers no biological warmth and her immortality disqualifies her as a heroic consort. Only Penelope shares Odysseus' intellectual alertness and is yet so alluring that she can represent the feminine counterpart of his heroic individuality. Whether or not we agree with the argument that in their conversation by the fireside in Book Nineteen Penelope consciously recognizes Odysseus,[9] we cannot doubt that at the least she senses intuitively the need to force a crisis with the suitors. Yet she will not acknowledge Odysseus later without testing him in her own terms; her equality as his partner is nowhere more convincingly displayed than in her subtle allusion to moving their bed. At the same time, there is no more vivid evidence of her spontaneous femininity than her touching surrender after Odysseus' angry response. Penelope embodies in attainable reality the combination of qualities which the Sirens imply in false illusion. Her depiction throughout the poem as Odysseus' loyal wife emphasizes that she alone can carry for him both the higher and the lower feminine values. In regaining Penelope, Odysseus reclaims something of his own soul and so makes meaningful his resistance to the wiles of all the other women he meets on his way home. Having avoided submitting to the powers of the unconscious in a way which would destroy his identity, he is able finally to relate to them in the only way which will complete it.

This achievement makes Odysseus one of the wholest men in literature. For Homeric man, both the spirit and the flesh are indispensable, and this is why Odysseus refuses the immortalities both of Calypso and of Hades. Put another way, man must be conscious to be human, but he must come to terms with the unconscious to be whole. Divided as we have been since Homer's time by our awareness of the duality of human nature, the *Odyssey* continues to impress us with its vital image of an integrated man.

VII

The Reunion of Odysseus and Penelope

ANNE AMORY

At Book Nineteen two main threads of the *Odyssey* merge, and the action begins to quicken toward its climax. Odysseus prepares and executes his revenge on the suitors, and his reunion with Penelope is accomplished by gradual stages. Dreams and omens play an increasingly important role as the climax of the poem approaches. In particular, Penelope's decision to set the contest of the bow, which is a pivotal point in both the revenge and reunion themes, cannot be understood except in terms of the omens and dreams which surround it.[1]

The interview between Penelope and Odysseus while he is still disguised as a beggar has been carefully prepared and artfully delayed,[2] but finally the two meet at the beginning of Book Nineteen. Penelope comes into the hall looking, the poet says, like Artemis or Aphrodite, and sits in the firelight on a chair inlaid with silver and ivory. She asks the stranger who he is and where he comes from, but Odysseus evades her questions and says instead that Penelope's fame has reached the wide heaven itself, like that of some perfect king whose people and country flourish under him (19.107–114). These words, the first to be spoken directly by Odysseus to his wife, are a good example of the way in which Homer invests his use of formulaic lines with special point and relevance.[3] Odysseus is several times described as a representative of the type of an ideal king, and he himself had told the Phaeacians that his fame reached heaven,[4] so his speech here is an acknowledgment that Penelope is worthy to be his wife. Moreover, his praise, being traditional, is indirect and apparently impersonal enough to be suitable to his role as a stranger, and yet extravagant enough to convey his natural excitement, which must be kept in check.

Odysseus was clearly always a master of subtle and intelligent praise, and we may well imagine that Penelope, who has heard nothing for a long time except her son's criticisms and the suitors' clumsy and rather offensive remarks, is pleased to be so addressed. She replies that the gods destroyed her beauty when Odysseus went to Troy, but that if he could return and take care of her, her fame would indeed grow greater and fairer. Her reply is formulaic also,[5] but just as clearly especially apposite here, for, since Odysseus has returned, she is actually accepting his praise in a way that must give him the deepest satisfaction.

Odysseus eventually tells her a false tale of who he is, and of how he had seen Odysseus on his way to Troy, whereupon Penelope breaks into tears. The preceding books have marked in detail the steps by which Penelope's habit of grief was gradually replaced with a painful turbulence as she simultaneously received indications that Odysseus was about to return and realized that Telemachus was now an adult and that she must therefore marry again.[6] Here the old pattern of feeling vanishes completely for the present, and the moment is marked by a simile: she weeps the way snow melts on the mountain peaks when the spring breezes thaw it (19.204–209). Odysseus is much moved by her distress, but hides his tears and keeps his eyes unblinking, like horn or iron.

Penelope questions the stranger about Odysseus' dress and appearance and, on hearing a true and detailed description, weeps again, but this time for a different reason. Previously, she has always wept simply for Odysseus' absence, not because she thought he was dead, for she had never allowed herself to form a conviction on that question. Now, however, her frozen grief has been dissolved, and the despair against which habitual mourning had been her only protection overcomes her. She weeps because she suddenly feels sure, in spite of all the recent assurances to the contrary, that Odysseus will not return (19.249–260).

The stranger at once assures her that Odysseus is safe and will return. He swears, in fact, just as Theoclymenus had done (17.155–

159), that he will appear shortly. Penelope says that she hopes he is right, using the same words she had used to Theoclymenus (19.309–311 = 17.163–165), but this time she goes on to say that she is still afraid that Odysseus will not come home. Nor, she adds, is there anyone so hospitable and competent as Odysseus was—if indeed Odysseus ever was,[7] for in her present despair her memory of him seems as illusory as the hope that he will return.

At this point there intervenes the famous episode in which the nurse Eurycleia recognizes Odysseus while washing his feet.[8] During the scene with Eurycleia, Penelope sits lost in thought; Athene, the poet says, occupied her mind with other things (19.479). She then gives the stranger an account of her feelings and situation. She describes her past sorrows and then passes to her present dilemma, using the myth of the nightingale as a complex image to express both (19.518–524).[9] She explains that her mind is divided between continuing to wait for Odysseus and marrying the best of the suitors. She says outright that Telemachus is now grown up and urging her to marry, but she is less direct about her reasons for wishing to delay a decision. She does not mention Theoclymenus' prophecy or the omen of Telemachus' sneeze;[10] instead she asks the stranger to interpret a dream for her (19.535 ff.).

In the dream, she says, an eagle swooped from the mountains and killed her pet geese; then he dropped from the sky again and explained that he was her husband who had returned and was about to take revenge on the suitors. Odysseus confirms this explanation of the dream's meaning, but Penelope is still dubious, for she thinks that this dream has come through the ivory gate of delusive dreams, not the gate of horn, through which true dreams come.[11] But then she abruptly announces that she has come to a decision and intends to choose one of the suitors very shortly by means of a contest with Odysseus' bow. The stranger urges her to do so and not to delay, for, he says, Odysseus will return before the suitors can string the bow (19.583–587).

It has often been asserted that Penelope's decision to set the contest of the bow is completely unmotivated as the poem stands. Separatists point out that a problem arises because her recognition of Odysseus has been transferred from before the revenge to afterward and conclude that only multiple authorship could explain such a serious and obvious "fault in the construction."[12] Unitarians sigh dolefully and admit that Homer here nods or resorts to naked interference with his characters because the contest is essential to his plot.[13]

It is undeniably true that the contest is necessary to the plot, and it is equally obvious that there would be no problem about Penelope's decision in a version which described the revenge as the outcome of a scheme framed by Odysseus and Penelope after she has recognized him. It is debatable, however, that Penelope's decision in our *Odyssey* has been left as completely implausible as scholars sometimes assert.

The only recent serious attempt to explain Penelope's motivation in the poem as we have it was made by Philip Harsh.[14] He argues that she actually recognizes Odysseus in Book Nineteen, but that her recognition must remain implicit because Odysseus cannot reveal his presence to the maidservants who are in the hall as they talk. In this reading of the scene, Penelope begins to suspect the truth when Odysseus describes in such detail the clothing he wore on departing for Troy. She then invents the dream during her reverie, in order to ask Odysseus, without arousing the maids' suspicions, if he intends to kill the suitors in the hall. Odysseus indicates that he does, by confirming the truth of the dream. Her skepticism is a reminder that the task will not be easy. Their last exchange, finally, arranges the method by which Odysseus is going to accomplish the revenge.[15]

Harsh's interpretation is ingenious, but it goes beyond the evidence to suppose that Penelope is so quickly certain of the beggar's identity, that the dream is a deliberate fabrication, and that her conversation with the beggar amounts to a definite agreement about a plan for slaying the suitors. Moreover, it has rightly been objected that Homer has a regular formula for indicating to the audience when a character is withholding information from another character: "thus he (or she) spoke, (while) thinking. . . ."[16] And if Penelope has fully recognized the stranger in Book Nineteen, why is she still so hesitant at the beginning of Book Twenty-three? Finally, Penelope's behavior in Harsh's interpretation is rather out of character. Harsh rightly remarks that Penelope, like Odysseus, "is ever on her guard against gods and men" and "insists on probing everyone" just as he does. He adds, however, that she is different from Odysseus "in that with feminine subterfuge she delays decisions until the situation has so clarified itself that no decision is necessary."[17] But if this is true, and most readers would agree that it is, Harsh is undermining his own theory, which requires Penelope to arrive very quickly at a definite decision about the beggar's identity and take immediate steps on the basis of that decision.

The true explanation of Penelope's behavior in Book Nineteen surely lies in the particular kind of perception which is characteristic of her. Odysseus looks at most things unwaveringly, as he does at Penelope's tears, and what he sees is immediately recognized by him as what it is; he sees what is actually around him and can reason explicitly about it. Penelope, on the other hand, looks at things only intermittently and thinks intuitively rather than rationally. She is always holding a veil in front of her face, or looking away from things, just as she does not notice Eurycleia's recognition of Odysseus. Odysseus knows what he knows, so he always doubts others, but never himself; once he has tested something, he is sure of it. But Penelope's knowledge is often unconscious; she doubts everything, including, or perhaps especially, what she herself has observed, in spite of the fact that her intuitive penetration is both profound and accurate.

This is not to say that Penelope lives in a perpetual daze of bewilderment about everything. In her interview with the stranger, one of the things on her mind is her situation in respect to the suitors and Telemachus, and on this subject she is entirely lucid and fully conscious of its implications. Those who feel that Penelope's decision to set the contest of the bow is inadequately motivated lay stress on the fact that she is not "being compelled to marry any suitor,"[18] for Telemachus repeatedly says that he will not force his mother to leave the house. It is essential, however, to look at the situation as it appears to Penelope and to believe the account which she gives to the beggar. She feels, accurately enough, that Telemachus would be glad if she remarried, whatever he may say about not forcing her to do so; she can see for herself that he has a right to his estate before the suitors ruin it completely; and she knows that the suitors have begun to think of killing Telemachus. However static the situation may have been in the preceding three or four years, it has changed radically since the poem began. For the first time since Odysseus' departure, a decision is urgent, as far as Penelope can see, in order to protect Telemachus' life and property. Thus far her thought process is quite conscious and she is therefore able to describe this side of her dilemma to the stranger in direct and straightforward terms.

The other side of her dilemma is formed by the problem of whether Odysseus will or will not return, and here Penelope's feelings are complex and, to a large extent, intuitive and subconscious. Accordingly, her account to the stranger becomes, when she touches on this aspect, indirect and allusive. She has that day received a number of omens which indicate that Odysseus is not only alive, but on the point of returning. She received them joyfully as they arrived, but a very strong current of pessimism is pulling her the other way. Dreams and omens may be wrong, and Penelope has especially good reason to fear that she may be deceived by them precisely because she hopes that they will prove true.[19] As a defense against this danger, she tries to tell herself that what she hopes is impossible. Hence her sudden conviction that Odysseus is dead, which is foolish from a rational point of view, but completely credible psychologically.

Meanwhile, she is actually face to face with the stranger, about whom she has already had one flash of hope, which she quickly repressed.[20] Now, as she talks with him, I suggest that Penelope becomes gradually certain that the stranger is in fact her husband. But, because she has so strong a fear of making a mistake in just this situation, she cannot rationally accept her interior certainty, and her recognition therefore remains largely subconscious. She does, however, test her intuition by a process of divination, familiar enough to the Greeks, but puzzling to modern readers: she solicits an omen. Sometimes a character in Homer uses this method of divination openly, as Priam does in the *Iliad* (24.308–321) when, at Hecabe's suggestion, he asks for an omen to confirm Iris' instructions that he go to Achilles, or as Odysseus does in Book Twenty. In this case there is no difficulty in understanding what is happening. But characters in Homer sometimes seek a sign indirectly, especially by saying the opposite of what they know or hope to be true, as Agamemnon does to test the dream from Zeus in Book Two of the *Iliad,* or as Telemachus does when he returns to Ithaca,[21] and then the significance may escape the reader who is not familiar with the practice of divination.

So here Penelope, in telling the beggar her dream, which epitomizes, as it were, all the other omens of Odysseus' return, is seeking a sign, not only to help her come to a decision about remarrying, but also to test her intuition that the stranger is himself Odysseus. He confirms her own interpretation of the dream,[22] but she is still afraid to believe it. She then puts forward her suggestion about setting the contest, in a state of conflict and confusion. She genuinely feels that a decision is necessary, but she is very reluctant to make one. Seeking a further sign, she makes her reluctance plain, so that the stranger can discourage her plan if he is not Odysseus, but is really sure that Odysseus is coming soon. But the stranger does not merely repeat his assurance that Odysseus will return; he urges her to go ahead with the contest immediately because Odysseus will be there before it is completed. This assurance is so peculiarly explicit[23] that Penelope must realize that Odysseus himself is speaking.

This leaves the poet, who has decided to postpone his recognition scene until after the contest, with the problem of preventing an immediate acknowledgment of Penelope's recognition, and this he does very adroitly and in complete consonance with Penelope's character as he has portrayed it. She makes no reply to the stranger's remarkable statement. She says simply that she must retire—to the bed where she has wept for Odysseus since he left, although she could talk to the stranger all night, if it were not that mortals have to sleep (19.588–599). That is, Penelope is not yet ready emotionally to accept Odysseus' return, so she does not admit her recognition of him, but just gives up the whole problem for the moment. Understandably, in view of the variety and intensity of the emotions which she has undergone that day, she is overcome by a sudden weariness and a desire to return to her old condition of passive waiting. This is marked by a repetition of the formula used several other times: she goes upstairs and weeps until Athene casts sweet sleep on her eyelids (19.603–604 = 1.363–364, 16.450–451, and 21.357–358).

At the beginning of Book Twenty, toward morning, Penelope wakes up and, just as she had done the day before (18.200–205), prays to Artemis for death. She wishes that she might vanish from the earth like Pandareus' daughters, to whom she had compared herself in Book Nineteen.[24] She explains that she would prefer to die with the image of Odysseus before her, rather than bring pleasure to a lesser man. It is bearable, she says, to weep all day if sleep brings forgetfulness at night, but now she has bad dreams. For she dreamed that Odysseus was with her, looking as he did when he went to Troy, and she rejoiced, believing that it was reality, not a dream (20.60–90).

Harsh comments on the "dramatic irony" of this speech, remarking that if she were to die now, "it would indeed be with Odysseus before her eyes." So much is certainly true, whether Penelope has fully recognized Odysseus or not. But if she has, as Harsh argues, why should she pray for death? He explains that she "lacks Odysseus' manly confidence in the outcome" of the contest and is afraid he will be killed by the suitors.[25] This is a possible explanation, but a rather feeble one, and Penelope's speech reveals a state of mind much more complex and ambiguous than Harsh supposes.

The three motifs which are repeated from previous scenes suggest that Penelope is attempting to retreat from the present into one or another of her earlier, less painful, attitudes. Each of these in turn proves impossible to recapture. Her first condition of habitual, mechanical grief is attainable only at the moment when she goes to bed. The old solace of peaceful nights is gone. Her prayer to Artemis, next, takes her back to the stage when her long dormant emotions were just beginning to be aroused by the omens prophesying Odysseus' return. In Book Eighteen she had prayed for death out of a desire to feel nothing, but now she can no longer hope for oblivion. The reference to Pandareus' daughters brings her up as far as the previous night to the point just before she had announced her decision to set the contest. Finally, by the time she repeats her wish for annihilation, she is completely back in the present, facing marriage to one of the suitors on one hand, and a full recognition of Odysseus on the other.

She is still not quite ready to accept either of these alternatives. She prefers to die rather than marry someone else; accepting Odysseus as he is now is also difficult. Her dream is much more intimate and poignant than the remote and undisturbing one she had in Book Four,[26] but in it she still sees Odysseus as he was twenty years ago. Her old love for him is thoroughly reawakened by this time, but that is a different matter from recognizing him as he is now and accepting the changes which his return inevitably entails.

Odysseus meanwhile is also dreaming of reunion. Only half awake, he hears Penelope weeping, and it seems to him in his heart (*kata thymon*) that she has already recognized him and is standing nearby, at his head (20.92–94). There has been some disagreement about the kind of mental experience described in these lines, but it seems clear enough that a dream, or the kind of early morning wishful imagining which is practically indistinguishable from a dream, is intended.[27] All of Odysseus' conscious mind is occupied with the problem of revenge; his feelings about Penelope, though strong, are temporarily submerged. When he hears her voice, he is just conscious enough to have his submerged desires appear undisguised and be fulfilled in imagination, but not awake enough to have remembered fully all the factors which prevent his desire from being fulfilled in reality.[28] This is the only insight we have into Odysseus' reaction to his interview with Penelope the night before, and it does not seem to support Harsh's reading of the scene. If Penelope had consciously and completely recognized Odysseus, he would have known it and have no need to be dreaming of it. As it is, it appears that Odysseus was aware of the ambivalence of Penelope's reactions, and, much as he would have appreciated her caution, his unfulfilled desire to be fully recognized by her emerges here in the interlude before the crisis with the suitors absorbs all his attention. And the juxtaposition of his dream with the corresponding one of Penelope's is an instance of that like-mindedness (*homophrosynē*) which existed between Odysseus and Penelope, and on which the poet constantly relies in his version of the reunion.

At this point, we must return to the revenge theme and pick up the thread of the omens which encourage Odysseus about his vengeance. The problem of killing the suitors is first broached upon Odysseus' return to Ithaca, when Athene assures Odysseus that she will stand by him (13.372 ff.). Then in his discussion with Telemachus Odysseus displays the greatest confidence about the favor of Zeus and Athene and the consequent success of his vengeance (see especially 16.260–261, 282, 297–298).

Later, however, Odysseus shows some anxiety about the outcome of his plans, and a series of omens reassures him. On the morning after Telemachus' return to Ithaca, Odysseus in his disguise as a beggar is taken to the palace by the faithful swineherd Eumaeus. On the way they meet the disloyal goatherd, Melanthius, who not only reviles them, but kicks at Odysseus. Eumaeus instantly prays to the nymphs, whose fountain they happen to be passing, that Odysseus may return and punish such a bad servant. Melanthius replies that he wishes he were as sure that Telemachus would perish as he is that Odysseus will not return (17.240–253).

To understand all the implications of this exchange it is necessary to know that the Greeks often regarded a speech as an omen. In particular, words which were capable of ambiguous interpretation because they were overheard or because of the speaker's ignorance of the true situation were regularly regarded as ominous. The technical term for such a speech is *klēdōn,* or *phēmē*.[29] Here Melanthius means to utter a bad omen for Telemachus, but since he does not realize that he is speaking to the already returned Odysseus, his words are actually a favorable omen for the success of Odysseus and Telemachus against the suitors.

Later, in the palace, the suitors instigate a fight between Odysseus and the regular palace beggar, Irus. When Odysseus wins, the suitors, in return for their amusement, wish that Zeus will grant the stranger whatever he desires, and Odysseus rejoices at the *klēdōn* (18.112–117).

The next sign of victory which Odysseus receives is the supernatural radiance shed by Athene's lamp while he and Telemachus are removing the arms from the great hall (19.1–46). This scene has long been a favorite battle ground for the separatists, and there are doubtless real difficulties about the way in which the removal of the arms is fitted into the plot as the poem stands now,[30] but the significance of the portent is clear enough. One of the Greek words for light, *phaos* (or *phoōs*), is regularly used metaphorically for "victory, salvation," etc. (as, for example, *Iliad* 6.6), and here the metaphor is fully expanded into a concrete dramatic scene, in accordance with a common Homeric practice.[31] Telemachus comments on the miracle (*mega thauma*) and Odysseus tells him to remember it, but does not expatiate on its meaning, which indeed is obvious enough both to Telemachus and to the audience.

Next Odysseus hears Penelope's dream, which is, from his point of view, an omen that he will succeed in killing the suitors. Not only is the dream itself an omen, but the incident which it contains closely resembles the bird omens which occur in the poem, except that it is perhaps even more obvious in its symbolism. An eagle swoops down from the mountain and kills Penelope's geese; they lie in heaps in the hall, just as the suitors will do, and the eagle soars into the clear sky (19.535–540).

Afterward, as Odysseus lies in the hall, he sees the maids going out to join the suitors and is tempted to try to kill them then and there. He represses this impulse, but lies awake pondering the problem of fighting against such odds. At last Athene appears to him and, though she does not give him any specific advice or assurance, she reminds him that she is a goddess and that with her help he could outwit fifty companies of men (20.45–51). She puts him to sleep, but he wakes shortly afterward, hearing Penelope, as described above.

Then Odysseus goes outside and prays to Zeus for signs. If it is with the gods' will that he has come home after so many sufferings, he wants someone within the house to utter a *phēmē,* and he wants a sign (*teras*) from Zeus outside (20.97 ff.). Zeus obligingly thunders from a clear sky, and Odysseus rejoices. The *phēmē* follows immediately. A mill woman who, being weaker than the rest, is still grinding her corn hears the thunder. She understands at once that it is a sign for someone and prays for herself as well. She wishes that the suitors who make her toil necessary should feast their last on that very day. Odysseus rejoices at both signs and feels confident that his vengeance is sure (20.120–121).

The mill woman's speech is not the most dramatic omen in the *Odyssey,* nor the most meaningful for the plot, but it holds a special place, for it touches a chord of common human sympathy which is absent from the others. All the omens in the *Odyssey* imply the operation of justice in the world, but in most of them the suitors' offences are represented as personal ones against Odysseus, his family, or their prerogatives. In this omen something more universal speaks—the just protest of the weak against the arrogantly strong—and through our sympathy with the woman we see the suitors' behavior in a context wider than their relation to Odysseus and their punishment as more thoroughly deserved.[32]

The next scene is parallel to the one with Melanthius in Book Seventeen. The cowherd Philoetius arrives and greets the stranger with the hope that good luck lies ahead of him in the future; he adds that he hopes Odysseus will return and put the unruly suitors to flight (20.199–225). In answer Odysseus gives him the same oath that he has given to Eumaeus and Penelope, that Odysseus will return shortly; he adds that Philoetius will see the suitors slain with his own eyes (20.230–234).

Such scenes as these are often misinterpreted through the very different religious conceptions which most readers naturally and unconsciously bring to the poems. Either their significance is overlooked entirely, because of unfamiliarity with the Greek habit of seeing signs of the gods' presence in the most trivial occurrences, or it is misinterpreted in various ways. Those who wish to rescue Homer from the common charge that his gods are devoid of any real religious meaning[33] often cite these passages as evidence that Homer did possess "spiritual quality and loftiness of religious ideas,"[34] but without entirely understanding the nature of the religious ideas.

In the Homeric poems the relation between gods and men is not only a convention of marvellous poetic power,[35] but reflects an intricate, subtle, by no means primitive view of man's psychology and of his position in the world both of other men and of nature.[36] The Olympian gods may represent various specific aspects of the natural world (Zeus, weather; Poseidon, sea, etc.) and of man as a physical being (Aphrodite, sexual passion; Athene, arts and crafts; Apollo, sickness and health, music, etc.). Taken together, they may represent the combination of circumstances and the interplay between circumstances and character in men's lives.

Moreover, the gods are intimately involved with the idea of heroism and with the action of heroic character in whatever world is appropriate to it. It is war in the *Iliad,* where the gods, Athene and Apollo especially, attend various heroes as concrete and dramatic symbols of the capacity of the heroes to achieve a godlike immortality (*kleos*) by the exercise of valor (*aretē*).[37] In the *Odyssey* there are two worlds: the folktale one of Odysseus' wanderings, where various minor divinities replace the usual Olympians;[38] and, secondly, the much more realistic world of Ithaca, where Zeus and Athene operate as visible symbols, Zeus of the justice and order to be re-established in Ithaca by the return of Odysseus, the rightful king, and Athene of the resourcefulness and intelligence that characterize not only Odysseus himself, but his whole family, his father Laertes included.[39]

It must be borne in mind that the Greek gods are seldom omnipotent and arbitrary deities who manipulate men or impose an external fate upon them. Instead they are part of the natural fabric of men's lives and, even though presented as anthropomorphic beings who interact with men in a direct way, they reflect, rather than control, the forces which govern all men. In Homer, then, omens and dreams foretell only what can reasonably be expected to issue from the way in which "merit and fortune are interrelated."[40] Thus the sequence of omens received by Odysseus in Books Twelve through Twenty, as described above, indicates that he will be victorious over the suitors because he is braver, more resourceful, and juster than they. The omens encourage him, similarly, because they reflect and confirm his own self-confidence.

The final and climactic prophecy of the suitors' doom occurs in the extraordinary scene at the end of Book Twenty. Telemachus rebukes the suitors sharply after one of them has hurled a cow's foot at the beggar. Another, Agelaus, concedes the justice of his rebuke, but goes on to suggest that Penelope should at last choose one of the suitors, since it seems obvious that Odysseus is never going to return. Telemachus replies that he has urged her to remarry, but will not compel her to do so. At these words Athene makes the suitors laugh, at first normally, but then hysterically.[41] The food they are eating seems to be sprinkled with blood, and their laughter changes to tears. Theoclymenus prophesies their death, with a vision of their ghosts going down to Hades. By now the suitors have returned to normal, and they laugh again because they think he is raving. He adds that not one of them will escape the evil that is coming upon them and departs (20.345–372).

This scene offers material for extensive comment,[42] but here we must confine ourselves to its effect on the other characters. Nothing whatever is said about Odysseus' reaction. The suitors are hardly conscious of what has happened, although the incident was an omen for them above all. Telemachus, however, clearly takes it as a signal that the revenge is about to begin, for he sits silently with his eyes fixed on Odysseus, waiting to see when he will begin the attack (20.385–386). Finally, Penelope is a witness of the scene; the poet goes out of his way to tell us that she had placed her seat where she would hear every word spoken in the hall.[43]

This last detail is clearly an important clue to Penelope's motivation, although its significance has usually been overlooked in discussions of her surrender. We left Penelope at the point where she had been encouraged by the stranger to hold the contest of the bow. She had tried to ignore her dilemma, finding it too dangerous and difficult, but it had pursued her even in sleep. Nothing has been said about her since, but it is a reasonable inference from what follows that she has stopped trying to come to a decision on rational grounds and determined to follow her instincts.

When she hears Theoclymenus' impressive prophecy of the suitors' doom, she evidently feels that the right moment has come, just as Telemachus does. They both realize that Theoclymenus' vision is a sign that the time for decisive action is near, but the difference in their reactions is instructive. Telemachus looks at his father for a signal, because he knows that Odysseus is planning an attack. Penelope, however, has no such definite information. She can only act on inspiration; and she must not only take the initial step which makes Odysseus' revenge possible, she must take it on her own initiative without any direct guidance from Odysseus, whereas Telemachus has only to follow his father's lead.

At this point, the poet cannot pause for a detailed explanation of Penelope's state of mind and reasons for deciding to set the contest now. He simply states that Athene inspired her to go and get the bow (21.1–2). For those who misunderstand the role of the gods in Homer, Penelope's decision here inevitably seems abrupt and unmotivated, and Athene's intervention appears an arbitrary resort to a *dea ex machina*. But Homer habitually objectifies internal mental processes in the figures of gods, and always with due regard for the psychological reality of his characters. Here Athene's intervention is a kind of shorthand for a psychological process at a moment when the narrative is too crowded to permit fuller presentation, but it also symbolizes the fact that Penelope, acting only on intuition, without a full knowledge of the situation, does just the right thing at the right time.[44]

There are several other indications in what follows that Penelope is acting without full conscious knowledge either of the situation or of her own emotions. When she takes down Odysseus' bow she weeps for a while, but no explanation of her tears is given, as it is on the other occasions when she weeps. It is not hard to furnish reasons. She weeps, in part, simply because the bow reminds her of Odysseus, just as Eumaeus and Philoetius weep when they see it (21.82–83). Sheer nervous tension, too, accounts for her tears, since she is committing herself to a course of action which is irrevocable, and about whose outcome she feels the utmost anxiety. Nonetheless, the absence of any stated reason suggests that Penelope herself does not entirely know why she weeps, because she does not really know how she feels.

Next, when she makes her announcement to the suitors, she does not give the reason which the suitors might expect—that she has at last given up hope of Odysseus' return. Instead she speaks rather as if she were calling the suitors' bluff. First she says they have feasted in Odysseus' house while he was absent and could not put forward any pretext except that they wished to marry her. Then without any transition, she simply goes on—"Come now, since the contest is ready" (21.73).

She watches silently while the suitors one after another try, and fail, to string the bow. Leodes, the first to try, speaks a word of ill omen for the suitors: "This bow will strip many good men of their life and soul" (21.153–154). Antinous replies angrily that he is talking nonsense, but Odysseus, Telemachus, and Penelope, who have understood the import of Theoclymenus' vision, would take Leodes' speech as a confirmatory *klēdōn*.

Eventually Odysseus, who has in the meantime disclosed himself to Eumaeus and Philoetius, comes forward and asks to try the bow so that he can see if any of his old strength remains. The suitors are afraid he may succeed (having seen him at work on Irus) and Antinous violently denies his request. But Penelope intervenes and tells Antinous not to insult Telemachus' guests. "Do you suppose," she goes on, "that the stranger will expect to marry me if he succeeds in stringing Odysseus' great bow? I am sure such a thought hasn't entered his mind" (21.312–317). Eurymachus replies that, of course, they do not expect the beggar to marry Penelope. But they are concerned about what the common people will say—that they have been unable to measure up to the man whose wife they are courting, while some poor beggar was easily able to string the bow (21.321–329).

Penelope retorts that they need not be so careful of their reputations, which have suffered already because of their disgraceful behavior. Even if the stranger should succeed, it would be no reflection on them, for he is big and well-built and claims to come of a noble family. She promises that if the stranger strings the bow she will give him clothes and arms and send him wherever he wishes to go.

Penelope's speeches are most delicately done and show to the best advantage on the assumption that her recognition of Odysseus is still mostly unconscious. If she has definitely recognized him, as Harsh thinks, her words seem a little bland; we expect a sharper edge of double meaning. If she has no suspicions of his real identity, as many scholars assume, they are too apropos. Even the pressing claims of Greek hospitality do not demand her lavish promises. And why should she champion the beggar's request at all, or why should the idea that he might marry her need disclaiming? He has only asked to string the bow, not to enter the contest. As it is, she hovers charmingly between saying almost too much and not quite enough.

What she says is the literal truth, as far as the action which will result from the contest is concerned. The beggar will not marry her, for he has done that already. She will furnish him with new clothes and arms, but they will be his own. She will send him where he wants to go, but he will not want to go anywhere, except to her—at least for the moment.[45] At the same time, her words are almost startlingly removed from the truth of what she will feel when she knows the result of the contest. This is a very curious state of affairs, appropriate only to the particular way in which the story is told in our *Odyssey*.

There is one other consideration that is often overlooked in assessing Penelope's reasons for setting the contest of the bow at this moment. The contest itself is a means of divination. One modern critic complains that Penelope might "just as well have invoked the chances of the lot."[46] Indeed she might, and with good reason, according to ancient belief. For subjecting an important choice to an apparently chance process, including that of drawing lots, was a regular means of ascertaining the will of the gods and insuring the right choice.[47] Hence Penelope, since her feelings are too complex and contradictory to guide her clearly, is doing the only safe thing in resorting to the contest. For if the omens are right, if the stranger had good reason for his advice, then she is doing exactly what Odysseus wants her to do. If, on the other hand, the omens are wrong and her trust in the stranger a result of self-deception, so that one of the suitors may win the contest, then she will at least be marrying a man who is the least inferior to Odysseus. If, that is, any one of the suitors succeeds; there is after all a good chance that none will, so that if Odysseus is neither present nor coming, the contest will prove merely another delaying device, as her web was in the original version of the story (see notes 46 and 55).

In the revenge theme, the stringing of the bow is itself an omen of success for Odysseus, for it assures him that his old prowess is still intact. This decisive moment is preceded by a *klēdōn,* marked by similes, and followed by an omen. The suitors make scornful remarks when Odysseus first picks up the bow; one wishes that the bow may be as likely to give him profit or delight (*onēsios*) as he is likely to succeed in stringing it (21.402–403). But Odysseus fits the string to the bow as easily as a bard strings his lyre, and the first arrow sings like a swallow. The suitors, at last realizing that their doom is at hand, turn pale, while Zeus thunders giving signs (*sēmata*), and Odysseus rejoices at the omen (*teras*).

When the battle begins, the long sequence of omens in the *Odyssey* is almost complete. There is only one more real omen, at the very end of the poem. Zeus hurls a thunderbolt to convince Odysseus that he must not continue the fight with the Ithacans (24.539–540). Zeus is the special protector of kings in Homer, and it is possible to interpret this omen as a symbol which marks the final supremacy of the true king returned.[48] On the other hand, the action of the end of the *Odyssey* is only sketched in rapidly, because the major significant themes have been completed. Zeus' thunderbolt accomplishes something that the poet wants in the action—which is the simplest function of omens in the narrative of Homer—and the symbolic overtones are only lightly sounded.[49]

Meanwhile there remains Athene's appearance during the slaying of the suitors. The incident is a perfect illustration and summary of the principles which govern the action of the gods in the Homeric poems. At a critical point in the battle Athene appears in the guise of Mentor, an old friend of Odysseus. Odysseus greets her joyfully, just as if he thought it was Mentor himself, but he knows, or suspects, that it is really Athene (22.210).[50] The suitors also address Athene as if she were Mentor, but without any suspicion of her real identity. She then turns to Odysseus and accuses him of being less brave now than he was at Troy fighting for Helen's sake, although he should be braver when fighting for his own possessions (22.226–235). The goddess does not bring immediate victory; she flies up to the roof, leaving Odysseus on his own. At this the suitors rally and attack. But Athene makes their spears miscarry, while helping Odysseus' party to hit their targets. Only at the very end does she raise her aegis and spread panic among the remaining suitors.

In this scene, Athene's speech represents Odysseus' own momentary fear of failure when his arrows are gone (21.147–149) and the way in which he regains his courage by reminding himself that he survived Troy and is now fighting for something more important to him personally.[51] Athene's appearance as Mentor represents the suitors' feeling that they will not be able to defeat Odysseus; her disappearance indicates their surge of confidence as they remind themselves of their far superior numbers and realize the weakness of Odysseus' position. Their confidence is overconfidence, however, and they miss their aim. The raising of the aegis is a sign of the decisive moment in any battle where one side breaks completely. The whole scene is a fine blending of the miraculous and the natural, and a good example of the economy of narrative and impressiveness of dramatic effect which epic gained by using the gods as it did.

The other theme, the reunion of Odysseus and Penelope, is brought to its conclusion in Book Twenty-three. No dreams or omens are involved, nor is there any divine intervention, except Athene's beautification of Odysseus, but the process by which Penelope recognizes Odysseus is itself a kind of divination. "Recognizes" is misleading, for if the interpretation offered above is correct, Penelope has already recognized Odysseus the night before. But in Book Twenty-three she must test her recognition, assure herself of the truth consciously, and admit openly that Odysseus is her husband, to herself as well as to him. The steps of this inner experience are explored in some detail, in contrast to the swiftness with which Penelope's decision to set the contest was narrated.[52]

Penelope was not present at the slaying of the suitors. As soon as she had successfully insisted that the beggar be given a chance to string the bow, Telemachus had ordered her to withdraw to her room and there, as usual, she wept until Athene put her to sleep (21.343–358). After the battle the nurse Eurycleia wakes her with the news that Odysseus is back and has killed all the suitors. Penelope complains that she has been awakened from the sweetest sleep she has had since Odysseus went to Troy and evinces the greatest skepticism about Eurycleia's news. Her essential belief is betrayed, however, by her indecision as to whether she should question her husband from afar or kiss him at once (23.85–87).[53] Nevertheless, when she gets to the hall she does neither. She simply gazes at Odysseus in silence, then looks away.

Odysseus remains patient throughout all these initial hesitations, but Telemachus is shocked at his mother's "hardheartedness." Odysseus, saying that she refuses to recognize him because of his squalor, bathes and puts on clean clothes. Here Athene intervenes and sheds miraculous beauty on him (23.156–162). This motif of divinely enhanced beauty is used several other times in the poem, always of Odysseus or one of his family.[54] It appears to be a symbol of Athene's special interest in them, and like most divine favors in Homer it has an adequate purely human explanation: the royal family of Ithaca clearly had the kind of looks which really impress a beholder only when the personality and intelligence which lie behind them become apparent. But the motif is regularly used to mark important moments and always impresses those who behold the effects. Penelope, however, comments neither on Odysseus' sudden access of beauty, nor even on the ordinary transformation wrought by the bath and clean clothes. The passage has consequently been condemned as an interpolation,[55] but again the poet is using a traditional motif for a special purpose. In common versions of the reunion, surely Penelope did recognize Odysseus as soon as he was cleaned up. But in our *Odyssey,* it is evident, her recognition of Odysseus is not to be based on external appearances. Hence also, in describing the reunion of Odysseus and Penelope, the poet ignores the external sign of the scar Odysseus received as a youth in the boar hunt, which had been sufficient proof of his identity for Eurycleia and the other servants. Similarly he was at pains to remove Penelope from the scene during the slaying of the suitors, so that she would not recognize Odysseus by his mastery of the bow.[56]

After Telemachus' outburst, Penelope tells him that she and Odysseus have signs (*sēmata,* the same word used of omens), which are secret and known to the two of them alone (23.107–110). Odysseus also uses the language of divination: "Let your mother," he tells Telemachus, "make trial of me" (23.113–114). When Penelope still refuses to recognize him after the bath, Odysseus is forced to take the first step in the revelation of their *sēmata.* He complains that Penelope is stubborn and that no other woman would have taken so long to recognize her husband. And to the nurse he says, "Come, spread my couch for me, so that I at least may go to bed. For she has an iron heart in her breast" (23.171–172). Penelope's response echoes his speech in form. First she replies to his criticism by saying that she doesn't mean to be willfully provoking; it is only that she has too clear an image of him as he was when he left: "I know very well what you were, leaving Ithaca" (23.175–176). Her use of the second person is a tacit admission that she knows she is speaking to Odysseus himself, but before he can seize on it, she continues, ordering Eurycleia to spread him a couch outside the chamber "which he himself built" (another tacit admission). "Thus she spoke," says the poet, "making trial of her husband" (23.181). At this point Odysseus, who has often lied and taken others in, is deceived enough by Penelope's falsehood to lose his temper (for the first time in the poem). He inquires angrily who has moved the bed which he himself built onto the trunk of an olive tree that grew like a pillar and describes the whole process in detail (23.182–204). It has often been remarked that Penelope is convinced as much by Odysseus' emotion as by his knowledge of the sign of the bed,[57] but it is less often observed that in eliciting his knowledge she uses the same technique of divination by opposites that she had applied to her dream in Book Nineteen (see above, page 105).

After Odysseus has met the test by describing their marriage bed in detail, Penelope surrenders completely. She asks him not to be angry and explains her initial hesitation. There was always a cold fear in her heart that a stranger might come and bewitch her with words. The jealous gods have kept them apart, the gods who tempted Helen to fall in love with a stranger. This speech (23.209–230), together with her earlier statement about her image of Odysseus when he left, provides a full illumination of Penelope's feelings and behavior in the earlier scenes of the poem as well. She failed to recognize Odysseus consciously for the same reasons that she hesitates to surrender openly here, and the reasons are completely credible psychologically. She could have maintained her love for Odysseus only by keeping her image of him unchanged and her emotions fixed in a habitual pattern; but both these processes entail the most difficult kind of readjustment at the end of the period of waiting. The danger of falling in love with a stranger—which Penelope epitomizes in the example of Helen—is also a perfectly real one in this situation.

The lines which refer to Helen have generally been condemned, from the time of Aristarchus to the present, on the grounds that they are immoral, irrelevant, and out of place. Even those who accept the lines as genuine misunderstand their import, for they assume that Penelope is defending her conduct with the suitors by contrasting herself with Helen.[58] But it is quite evident from the poem that Odysseus is not angry at Penelope's behavior with the suitors,[59] and Penelope herself is clearly referring only to her delay in admitting that Odysseus is her husband.

As often in Penelope's speeches, the logical connections are somewhat obscure and indirect, but scholars have been curiously obtuse in interpreting this speech. First of all, they assume that what Penelope must mean is that an impostor might have convinced her that he was Odysseus. Then, of course, the example of Helen is not strictly parallel. But what Penelope actually says is merely that a stranger might have "beguiled" her. That is, she was afraid she might fall in love with someone else, as Helen did with Paris. It is important, also, to understand clearly what is expressed by Penelope's references to the gods in this speech. When she says that the gods begrudged them the chance to enjoy their life together from youth to old age (23.210–212), the gods signify events, the circumstances which man must accept, since he cannot control them. When she says that a god made Helen unfaithful (23.222), the gods represent human nature and the frailness of its defences against self-deception, desire, and loneliness.

Penelope's speech, then, is not just an excuse for her failure to recognize Odysseus immediately. It is a comment on the whole meaning of their separation. It shows that she understands both the causes and the consequences of such situations in general. In particular, it shows that Penelope has not been faithful to Odysseus out of sheer unimaginativeness. Her words tell Odysseus that although she was fully aware of the dangers that their separation entailed, she had enough love and courage, and enough of his own caution and endurance, to enable them to be safely reunited. Odysseus does not answer Penelope in words, but the poet makes his reaction perfectly clear: "He wept, holding his cautious wife who fitted his heart (*thymarea*)" (23.232).

Notes

Some references in the notes printed originally with certain of the essays have been enlarged in order to make them clearer to the reader who is not a specialist.

I. *Gods and Men in Homer*

1. V. Ehrenberg, inaugural lecture at Prague, 1929, reprinted in *Aspects of the Ancient World* (Oxford, 1946), p. 4.

2. If the Homeric poems were composed by people quite unconscious of being teachers and innocent of the intention, this does not make the use of the word any less appropriate. We are dealing with the effect of the poems, not the intentions of the bards.

3. See chapter ten, part six, *The Greeks and Their Gods.*

4. See especially H. J. Rose, *Modern Methods in Classical Mythology* (St. Andrews, 1930), pp. 13 ff.

5. *Od.* 4.63; Rose, *Mod. Meth. Class. Myth.*, p. 14.

6. I owe this point to the book of Professor Bruno Snell of Hamburg, *Die Entdeckung des Geistes* (Hamburg, 1946). Snell's choice of words in commenting on the passage seems exactly right: "Welch vornehme Liebenswürdigkeit liegt in diesen drei kurzen Worten [εἴ κε πίθηαι, line 207]. Solches Sprechen setzt aristokratische Gesellschaftsformen voraus: höflich und ritterlich nimmt einer Rücksicht auf den anderen und zügelt die eigenen Ansprüche."

7. *Od.* 22.169 ff., 465 ff. See Rose, *Mod. Meth. Class. Myth.*, p. 13.

8. Rose, *ibid.*, and *A Handbook of Greek Mythology* (London, 1928), pp. 80 ff.

9. Herodotus, *History* 1.32, trans. Rose.

10. *Il.* 6.146 ff.

> οἵη περ φύλλων γενεή, τοίη δὲ καὶ ἀνδρῶν.
> φύλλα τὰ μέν τ' ἄνεμος χαμάδις χέει, ἄλλα δέ θ' ὕλη
> τηλεθόωσα φύει, ἔαρος δ' ἐπιγίγνεται ὥρη.
> ὣς ἀνδρῶν γενεὴ ἡ μὲν φύει, ἡ δ' ἀπολήγει.

11. *Od.* 11.489 ff.

12. Martin P. Nilsson, *Mycenean and Homeric Religion* (a lecture de-

livered in Cambridge and Manchester, 1936, and published in *Beitr. zur Religionswiss. der religionswiss. Ges. zu Stockholm*), p. 85; *A History of Greek Religion* (Oxford, 1925), p. 146.

13. Nilsson, *Hist. Gr. Rel.*, p. 152.

14. That this was the once prevailing view about the gods, which was only with difficulty superseded in a more philosophic age by a different conception, is well illustrated by the question seriously debated in the *Euthyphro* of Plato, whether righteous acts are righteous because the gods love them or the gods love them because they are righteous.

15. *Od.* 4.689 ff.; 14.58 ff.; 11.218; 19.167; 24.254 f. The old sense was of course preserved in the later adverbial use of the accusative to mean "like," "after the manner of."

16. Or "low." The word may have been αἰσχρόν or φαῦλον. The line is frag. 294.7, *Tragicorum Graecorum Fragmenta,* ed. A. Nauck (2nd ed. Leipzig, 1889), from Euripides' *Bellerophontes.*

17. *Od.* 24.351 f.

18. It would not however have been difficult to quote passages from the *Odyssey* illustrating the "higher" morality also. Nilsson has done so (*Hist. Gr. Rel.* p. 153), and adds: "But it is significant that these passages occur in the *Odyssey.*" In my view there is no significance in this at all.

19. *Il.* 16.384 ff.

20. Nilsson, *Hist. Gr. Rel.,* p. 153. Leaf, we must admit, argued that lines 387–389 are an interpolation by "a poet of the Hesiodean school." See his note *ad loc.*

21. An addendum to the discussion of the word *dike* may be of interest. Plato wrote his greatest work ostensibly for no other purpose than to discover what it (or its close correlative *dikaiosyne*) meant. Are we sometimes disappointed at the mouse-like result which finally emerges after his mountains of discussion? It is nothing more than τὰ ἑαυτοῦ πράττειν, to act in the way that is properly your own and not another's. The conclusion has a certain added interest when it appears that what Plato has done is to reject the meanings of the word which were current in his own day, and from which we have taken our translation of it as *justice,* and, with a historical sense that was doubtless unconscious, to go back to its original sense. It is rooted in the old Homeric idea of strict class-distinctions, and class-distinctions were the mainstay of Plato's aristocratic state.

For *dike* cf. now L. R. Palmer, *The Indo-European Origins of Greek Justice, Trans. Philol. Soc.* 1950, pp. 149–168.

II. *Personal Relationships*

1. Menelaus speaks of Odysseus with affection in *Od.* 4.169 ff., but that was nine years after the fall of Troy. He shows no signs of special friend-

liness to him in the *Iliad*. Ajax's words in *Il*. 9.642, do not imply any special intimacy. There is a statement in *Od*. 19.247, that Odysseus honored his herald Eurybates above all his companions because he "saw eye to eye" (Rieu) with him. Eurybates is signalized there with a remarkable description, and one feels he had a significant part in some version of the legend; but Homer says nothing more of him. Eustathius *ad loc*. tells some extraordinary tales about him: cf. *Paulys Real-Encyclopädie der Classischen Altertumswissenschaft* (VI, Stuttgart, 1909) at "Eurybates."

2. Odysseus' loneliness is not specially emphasized in the classical tradition. It becomes a dominant feature in his characterization by Fénelon, Tennyson, Pascoli, and Joyce.

3. *Il*. 2.260; 4.354.

4. *Il*. 2.292 ff. The Venetus B scholiast regards this passage as a prelude to the affection of Odysseus and Penelope as portrayed in the *Odyssey*, i.e., as a piece of "poetic economy."

5. Eustathius in his introduction to the *Od*. 6 distinguishes the erotic love of Circe and Calypso from the affection of Athene which is based on the pleasure of dealing with an intelligence and wisdom like her own. The earliest insinuation that Athene was amorous of Odysseus is, so far as I know, made by Poseidon in Stephen Phillips' *Ulysses*: see chapter fourteen.

6. The tragic potentialities of this licence are exemplified in the case of Phoenix (*Il*. 9.449). Teucer also was an illegitimate son (*Il*. 8.286).

7. That is so far as Homer's narrative goes; the *argumentum ex silentio* is supported by Odysseus' known characteristics and conduct. The Venetus A scholiast on *Il*. 1.182, and the B and Townleian scholiasts on *Il*. 1.138, say that Laodice, the daughter of Cycnus, was allotted to Odysseus. Athenaeus (*Deipnosophistae* 13.556D), discussing illegitimate children, cites Aristotle (*Fragmenta*, ed. V. Rose, Leipzig, 1886, frag. 162) for the statement that only Menelaus was without a concubine at Troy; but Aristotle seems to have explained the problems involved by suggesting that most of the women slaves awarded to the various heroes (including Nestor) were "as an honor" (εἰς γέρας) not "for use" (εἰς χρῆσιν).

8. This view is presented in Plutarch's *Bruta animalia ratione uti* (*Gryllus*): the transformed men give reasons for preferring to remain animals. This Cynic paradox became influential in the vernacular tradition after Gelli's version of the Circe legend in 1548: see E. M. W. Tillyard, *The Elizabethan World Picture* (London, 1943), p. 26.

9. *Od*. 10.472: the companions begin, δαιμόνι' ἤδη νῦν μιμνήσκεο, which can be colloquially rendered "You're a surprising man. Isn't it about time that you remembered . . . ?" Calderon in his *Love the greatest enchant-*

ment emphasizes the difficulty of freeing Odysseus from Circe's fascinations: see chapter fourteen.

10. It was not always so, as Homer's discreet remark in *Od.* 5.153 implies: "since the nymph *no longer* delighted him."

11. The symbol of the smoke from Odysseus' hearth fire became a favorite motif in the later tradition: cf. Ovid, *Epistles,* 1, 3, 33–34, du Bellay's sonnet *Heureux qui comme Ulysses,* and the "azure pillars of the hearth" in Tennyson's *Princess.* Clement of Alexandria (*Exhortation to the Gentiles* 25) remarks that Odysseus should have yearned for the radiance of the Heavenly City rather than for a mere wisp of mundane smoke.

12. Cf. L. A. Post, *From Homer to Menander* (Berkeley, 1951), p. 14: "a united family is the goal."

13. Cf. Lucian, *Vera historia* 2.29, where Odysseus secretly sends a letter from Ithaca to Calypso; cf. Philostratus, *Life of Apollonius* 7.10.

14. I owe this interpretation to Müller's imaginative study in the symbolism of the Odyssean voyages (H. Müller, *Odysseus, Mann, Seele und Schicksal,* 2nd ed., Chemnitz Brunner, 1932).

15. Homer repeats that Odysseus' liaison with Calypso was "perforce" in *Od.* 4.557; 5.14; and he uses the verb "held back" (κατέρυκε) in 1.55; 23.334. Is it accident or a stroke of subtle policy that Odysseus does not refer to any such compulsion on Calypso's part, in his speeches to the Phaeacians (7.244 ff.; 12.448 ff.)?

16. See E. F. D'Arms and K. H. Hully, "The Oresteia Story in the *Odyssey,*" *Transactions of the American Philological Society* LXXVII (1946), 207–213. They note parallels and contrasts between Odysseus and Agamemnon, Penelope and Clytaemnestra, Telemachus and Orestes, the suitors and Aegisthus. Their view that Homer intended these implicit comparisons to ennoble the "provincial" royalty of Ithaca is questionable.

17. J. W. Mackail in *Love's Looking-glass* (London, 1891).

18. Woodhouse (to whose analysis I am much indebted in what follows). (W. J. Woodhouse, *The Composition of Homer's Odyssey,* Oxford, 1930.)

19. Plutarch (*Quomodo adulescens,* 27) admits that Nausicaa's wish that "such a man as this should dwell here and be my husband" (*Od.* 6.244–245) would be bold and licentious, if uttered without a knowledge of Odysseus' good character (which, he assumes, she has already got by observation and intuition).

20. *Od.* 8.457 ff.

21. Cf. Woodhouse, *Composition of Homer's Odyssey,* p. 64: "Who does not feel that there is something hard and unsatisfying in this ending of her first passion? We feel perhaps just a little sorry that, after all, there is

a Penelopeia patiently waiting in the background. In the original old story . . . here so sadly mutilated and dislocated, everything went as the heart would have it." Cf. Post, *Homer to Menander,* p. 22. The theory that Nausicaa was originally a typical fairyland princess whose role in the pre-Homeric tradition was to be wooed and won by a mysterious stranger was first developed, as far as I know, by van Leeuwen's article in *Mnemosyne* XXXIX (1911), reprinted with additions in his *Commentationes Homericae* (Leyden, 1911). W. R. Paton added further possibilities in *The Classical Review* XXVI (1912), 215–216. Some of the arguments offered in its favor are unconvincing, as when Paton says that Odysseus' hot bath in *Od.* 8.449 ff., is "obviously the wedding bath"—but what is more natural than that a man should bathe before a public banquet, after a day at an athletic contest and among a people whose love of hot baths was unusually great?

22. Goethe in the fragments of his unfinished play, *Nausikaa.*

23. Mackail, *Love's Looking-glass.*

24. For references to the fact that Penelope yearned for Odysseus and hated her life without him see *Od.* 16.37–39; 17.272–274; 19.136.

25. This interpretation was already known in antiquity: see Seneca, *Epistulae Morales* 88.8. For arguments in its favor see P. W. Harsh, "Penelope and Odysseus in *Odyssey* XIX," *American Journal of Philology* LXXI (1950), 1 ff.; cf. Post, *Homer to Menander,* pp. 24 and 275. But R. Merkelbach, *Untersuchungen zur Odyssee* (Munich, 1951), p. 237, argues that if Homer had intended this subtlety he would have said so explicitly, e.g., "But she knew in her heart that it was Odysseus."

26. *Od.* 19.103 ff.: especially 115 ff., 166, 209 ff.

27. *Od.* 23.85 ff. In what follows I discuss especially 113 ff., 156 ff., 174 ff., 209 ff.

28. Cf. Post, *Homer to Menander,* p. 23: "It is not merely Odysseus' knowledge of the secret that assures Penelope of his identity; his righteous indignation discloses a passion that she recognizes."

29. The element of paradox: Eustathius on *Od.* 19.488.

30. Eustathius on *Od.* 23.110 ff. At times his urbane humanism resembles that of another famous prelate who interpreted the Ulysses story, Fénelon, Archbishop of Cambrai.

31. πεπνυμένος.

32. Notably Fénelon in his *Télémaque* and James Joyce in *Ulysses.* Tennyson in his *Ulysses* makes Odysseus rather contemptuous of his "most blameless" son.

33. *Od.* 24.244 ff.

34. *Od.* 24.240: πρῶτον κερτομίοισ' ἐπέεσσιν διαπειρηθῆναι.

35. The scholiast on *Od.* 11.177, suggests that Odysseus, aware that mothers-in-law usually dislike their daughters-in-law, tactfully left his in-

quiry about Penelope to the end; and that Anticleia, wishing to please her son, answered that question first. But Aristarchus took the reversal in the order simply as an example of Homeric hysteron proteron, which may be right. Cf. *Oxyrhynchus Papyri* VIII, 1086.16 ff.

36. Tributes from Eumaeus in *Od.* 14.62 ff., 137 ff. (147 implies a special degree of friendly veneration), 167 ff.

37. *Od.* 7.237–239.

III. *The Odyssey and the Western World*

1. Author of *Allegoriae Homericae,* which apparently belongs to the Age of Augustus. Reprinted in Leipzig (1910) as *Heracliti Quaestiones Homericae.*

IV. *The Name of Odysseus*

1. This quotation is from E. V. Rieu's excellent translation. So, in whole or in part, are many of the passages which follow.

2. Aeschylus, *Agamemnon* 182–183 (Lattimore's translation).

V. *Calypso and Elysium*

1. Following an earlier suggestion of Nitzsch, E. Rohde, *Psyche* (Leipzig, 1894) pp. 63 ff., considered the reference to Menelaus' future in 4.561 ff. as a later interpolation. His skeptical argument was considerably amplified by P. Capelle, "Elysium und Inseln der Seligen," *Archiv f. Religionswiss.* XXV (1927), 245–264 and XXVI (1928), 17–40. On the other hand, many students of Greek religion have insisted that the concept of the afterlife which is represented in Proteus' prophecy springs from an earlier phase of Greek thought, long antedating Homer. Cf. L. Malten, "Elysion und Rhadamanthys," *Arch. Jahrb.* XXVIII (1913), 35 ff.; M. Nilsson, *Minoan-Mycenean Religion* (Lund, 1927), pp. 540 ff. and *Geschichte der Griechischen Religion* (Munich, 1941), I, pp. 302 ff.; and finally W. K. C. Guthrie, *The Greeks and Their Gods* (Boston, 1956), pp. 290–291. In general, the latter view has prevailed.

2. The episode with Calypso has also suffered attack, on the grounds that it contains useless repetition of the Circe episode, which itself must be considered original. Cf. Wilamowitz' *Homerische Untersuchungen* (Berlin, 1884), p. 116. In reply to this criticism, one can question the fact of Circe's priority over Calypso in the original journey of Odysseus: cf. W. Kranz, "Die Irrfahrten des Odysseus," *Hermes* L (1915), 93–112. One can also question whether in fact Calypso only repeats motifs from Circe: cf.

H. Güntert, *Kalypso* (Halle, 1919), pp. 9 ff. The best general information on Calypso will be found in the article by H. Lamer in *Paulys Real-Encyclopädie der classischen Altertumswissenschaft* (x, part 2, Stuttgart, 1919). He, too, opposed Wilamowitz. Lamer differentiated Elysium and Ogygia (col. 1788), and I shall argue against that conception. Some useful discussion of Calypso will be found in D. J. Snider, *Homer's Odyssey: A Commentary* (Chicago, 1895).

3. Cf. Güntert and Lamer.

4. V. Bérard, *Calypso et la mer de l'Atlantide* (Paris, 1929), identified Ogygia with Peregil, a small island off North Africa. He observed also what Eustathius long ago had noted in his commentary, that Calypso as daughter of Atlas, Atlantis, inhabits an island which in location and general associations bears close resemblance to the Atlantis described by Plato in *Critias.*

5. Cf. Capelle (see note 1). He comments especially on Hesiod's description of the Isles of the Blessed in *Works and Days,* 169 ff. and Pindar's picture of the afterlife in *Olympian Odes,* 2.68 ff.

6. Cf. *Helen* 1677.

7. Cf. the Roman tradition of the *insulae divites* or *fortunatae,* often identified with the Canary Islands, as in Strabo, *Geography,* 1.1.5 and Pliny, *Natural History,* 6.202, or vaguely located in the unexplored Atlantic: cf. Horace, *Epode* 16 and Diodorus, *Library of History,* 5.19.

8. Our earliest information on Sertorius' project comes from the near-contemporary Sallust, frag. 100 of his *Historiae.* The full story will be found in Plutarch's *Sertorius* 8. Sertorius clearly hoped to sail from Spain out into the Atlantic.

9. Cf. Lamer (see note 2). Our earliest evidence consists of a fragment of Hesiod quoted by the scholiast at *Od.* 1.83. Ogylos off Crete was long favored. Apollonius Rhodius, *Argonautica,* 4.574 places Calypso on the island of Nymphaea off Epirus. Roman writers liked islands off southern Italy: cf. Pliny, *Natural History,* 3.96. Dio Cassius, *Roman History,* 48.50 places Calypso at Lake Avernus.

10. *Geography,* 1.2.18.

11. In accordance with Calypso's directions, Odysseus holds a steady course by keeping Orion and the Bear on his left hand (5.271 ff.); which means that he sails from west to east. The steady, balmy wind which the nymph gives him (268) resembles the continuous zephyr which passes over Elysium. Cf. Kranz (see note 2), p. 93.

12. It has been observed that on a clear day visibility in the Mediterranean extends to one hundred miles. Cf. E. C. Semple, *The Geography of the Mediterranean Region: Its Relation to Ancient History* (New York, 1931), pp. 586 ff.; and M. Cary, *The Geographical Background of Greek*

and Roman History (Oxford, 1949), pp. 29 ff. Both books point out, furthermore, that no easy west wind blows steadily, but the wind for navigation is a northeasterly tradewind. No island in the Mediterranean is 100 miles from another point of land; and Bérard's Peregil (note 4) lies within 10 miles of the African coast. It could be argued that Homer did not possess such accurate geographical data on the western Mediterranean, but, even so, he was describing an imaginary site, outside the experience of the Greek mariner.

13. Güntert (see note 2), p. 172.

14. Pp. 29 ff.

15. Pp. 167 ff.

16. Pp. 170 ff.

17. Cf. Circe's description of these glades in 10.510.

18. Güntert, p. 171.

19. Pp. 182 ff.

20. Cf. the useful remarks of E. Abrahamson, "The Adventures of Odysseus," *Classical Journal* LI (1956), 313–316.

21. Cf. A. Parry, "Landscape in Greek Poetry," *Yale Classical Studies,* XV (1957), 24: "Odysseus is in this landscape, or on the edge of it; but he will not give in to its blandishments."

22. D. Page, *The Homeric Odyssey* (Oxford, 1955), p. 72.

23. The only ancient writer known to me to introduce Odysseus into Elysium is Lucian in that ironically named *True Story* of his. Since he openly sets out to mock the fantasies of Homer and Herodotus, one might well argue *per contra* that, if Lucian placed Odysseus after death on the Blessed Isles, then he definitely did not belong there in popular and literary tradition. Cf. Lucian, *True Story* 2.5 ff. In the same way, Lucian makes Odysseus write to Calypso expressing regret that he ever left her (29 and 35).

VI. *The Obstacles to Odysseus' Return*

1. Cedric H. Whitman, *Homer and the Heroic Tradition* (Cambridge, Mass., 1958), p. 296.

2. W. B. Stanford, *The Ulysses Theme: A Study in the Adaptability of a Traditional Hero* (Oxford, 1954), p. 215. See also chapter four, reprinted above.

3. In the next several paragraphs, I examine individually the encounters of Odysseus with the agents who delay his return to Ithaca. A number of the observations I make have been suggested or implied by other critics. George Dimock ("The Name of Odysseus," reprinted above) especially has developed with care Odysseus' concern for his identity, though my inter-

pretations of certain episodes, notably the encounters with Polyphemus, the Laestrygonians, and the Sirens, differ significantly from his. I give my own readings of the several episodes together in order to make clear the perspective upon which my extension of previous readings in the latter half of this essay depends.

4. See W. K. C. Guthrie, *The Greeks and Their Gods* (Boston, 1950), chapter two, part six; Walter F. Otto, *The Homeric Gods,* trans. Moses Hadas (New York, 1954), pp. 27–28; U. von Wilamowitz-Moellendorff, *Der Glaube der Hellenen* (2 vols., Berlin, 1931–32), I, 212 ff.; and Paul Kretschmer, "Zur Geschichte der griechischen Dialekte," *Glotta,* I (1909), pp. 27–28.

5. See Stanford (ed.), *The Odyssey* (2 vols., London, 1947–48), *ad loc.*

6. Bruno Snell, *The Discovery of Mind: the Greek Origins of European Thought,* trans. T. G. Rosenmeyer (Oxford, 1953), chapter one.

7. E. R. Dodds, *The Greeks and the Irrational* (Berkeley, 1951), p. 40. In the foregoing discussion I am indebted to chapters one and two.

8. Erich Neumann, *The Origins and History of Consciousness* (New York, 1954), p. 340, n. 15.

9. This is the argument of Philip W. Harsh, "Penelope and Odysseus in *Odyssey* XIX," *American Journal of Philology,* LXXI (1950), 1–21. But see Anne Amory, "The Reunion of Odysseus and Penelope," below.

VII. *The Reunion of Odysseus and Penelope*

1. This article is a chapter of a projected book on divination in the *Odyssey.*

2. Those who believe that Penelope's appearances in Books Sixteen and Eighteen are interpolations have not reflected how much less meaningful Book Nineteen would be with those scenes absent.

3. Nevertheless it has been objected that these lines are "not quite in place," and Hesiodic "in substance and style"; see D. B. Monro, *Homer's Odyssey XIII–XXIV* (Oxford, 1901), *ad loc.*

4. 9.20; he is described as a representative of the type of the ideal king by Athene in 5.8–12, by Eumaeus in 14.61–66, and 14.137 ff., and by Philoetius in 20.204–210.

5. She had made the same reply to Eurymachus; 19.124–129 = 18.251–256. Albert B. Lord, *The Singer of Tales* (Cambridge, Mass., 1960), especially pp. 30–67, is the fullest and most recent exposition of the substance and implications of Milman Parry's work on the formulaic nature of the Homeric poems.

6. At the beginning of the poem Penelope is in a state of suspended animation, as it were. Her grief for Odysseus has become a habitual pat-

tern, but not really very painful (see, e.g., 1.343–344 and 4.832–837). The first break comes when she confronts the suitors after learning of their plot to kill Telemachus (16.409 ff). Next she is deeply stirred by the interview with Telemachus and Theoclymenus (17.150 ff.) and by Eumaeus' account of the newly arrived beggar (Odysseus in disguise) (17.528 ff.). Finally there is the controversial scene in which Penelope extracts gifts from the suitors (18.158 ff.). It is here, in my opinion, that Penelope for the first time suspects that the beggar may be Odysseus himself.

7. *ei pot' eēn ge* (19.315), a regular formula, apparently, for a past that seems irrecoverable; cf. Helen in the *Iliad* (3.180).

8. Cf. Erich Auerbach, *Mimesis* (Princeton, 1953), pp. 3–23 for a detailed analysis of this scene.

9. She grieves as the daughter of Pandareus grieved for her son Itylus, and her mind turns hither and thither the way the melody of the nightingale's song changes. For appreciative comments on this speech see W. J. Woodhouse, *The Composition of Homer's Odyssey* (Oxford, 1930), p. 86 and J. W. Mackail, "Penelope in the *Odyssey*," *Classical Studies* (New York, 1926), pp. 63–67.

10. 17.155–161 and 17.541–550; cf. note 6 above.

11. Her doubt is expressed in the famous and much imitated speech about the gates of horn and ivory (19.560–569). See E. L. Highbarger, *The Gates of Dreams* (Baltimore, 1940).

12. Cf., for example, Denys L. Page, *The Homeric Odyssey* (Oxford, 1955), pp. 123–124 and 128–130.

13. Cf., for example, Woodhouse, pp. 80–91.

14. Philip Whaley Harsh, "Penelope and Odysseus in *Odyssey* XIX," *American Journal of Philology*, LXXI (1950), 1–21.

15. There is a minor point which supports Harsh's thesis, although he does not mention it. It does not seem likely that Penelope would have had such a dream until after she had received some indication that Odysseus was alive and would return. But all the signs she has received have occurred only since that morning, when Telemachus returned, so that the only time she could have had the dream is during her brief sleep in 18.187–200, a moment already crowded by Athene's application of divine cosmetics. However, no listener or casual reader is likely to notice the chronological discrepancy, and it seems best to accept the dream as a genuine one.

16. As Odysseus does, when Athene appears during the slaying of the suitors. Cf. W. B. Stanford, *The Ulysses Theme* (Oxford, 1954), p. 253, note 25.

17. Harsh, p. 4.

18. Cf. Woodhouse, pp. 81–82. Telemachus says (20.341–344) that although he will not compel her to marry, he does suggest (*keleuō*) that she should, but this is after he knows that his father is back. Telemachus is outwardly portrayed as a dutiful son, but it is clear that he and Penelope do not get on well, for Telemachus is throughout secretive, peremptory, and critical when he is with her.

19. This is easily inferred here; Penelope expresses the same fear openly to Odysseus in 23.208 ff. Cf. the way in which Odysseus is reluctant to believe that he is at last back in Ithaca (13.324–326), and Telemachus that the stranger is really his father (16.194–200).

20. In 18.158 ff. when, if I am correct (see note 6), Penelope appears in the hall because she has a sudden and totally irrational (as it seems to her) flash of hope that the beggar may be Odysseus himself.

21. See Cedric H. Whitman, *Homer and the Heroic Tradition* (Cambridge, Mass., 1958), p. 341, note 13.

22. Penelope professes not to know at all what the dream means, but she herself dreams the (correct) interpretation which is offered by the eagle-Odysseus figure in the dream. For a discussion of the way in which successive dreams or portions of a dream often become "bolder and more distinct" in revealing their symbolic meaning, see Sigmund Freud, "The Interpretation of Dreams," in *The Basic Writings of Sigmund Freud* (Modern Library, 1938), pp. 357–358.

23. Especially 19.585–587. Harsh, p. 17, thinks that these lines are ambiguous, for they "could mean that the suitors will never string the bow." But in context the words would more naturally be taken literally, and the only way the stranger could reasonably be sure that Odysseus would appear in the midst of the contest is by being Odysseus himself.

24. Monro, *ad loc.,* rightly remarks that "the two passages have the air of belonging to different myths," but this passage would still remind the hearer of the one in 19.518 ff.

25. Harsh, p. 18.

26. 4.795 ff., where Telemachus is more on her mind than Odysseus. She does ask the dream figure (her sister, sent by Athene) whether Odysseus is alive or dead, but appears more comforted than distressed by the dream's evasive reply.

27. For one thing, Penelope stands in the conventional position, at the head of the sleeper, for a dream in Homer. For the view that this is a "*waking* impression" see Monro, *ad loc.*

28. Dreams in Homer are regularly wish-fulfillment dreams; cf. in the *Iliad* Agamemnon's dream at the beginning of Book Two and Achilles' dream of Patroclus in 23.62 ff.

29. The first is often written *kleēdōn* in epic. G. Autenrieth, *Homeric*

Dictionary (London, 1886) tries to distinguish in meaning between the two terms, but they are clearly used interchangeably in Homer, as in 20.97 ff.

30. See, e.g., Monro, *ad loc.,* Woodhouse, pp. 158–171, and Page, 92–100. The solution to this problem, as to so many other Homeric *cruces,* lies in the conflation of different versions by one poet, rather than in the assumption of interpolation by different poets. Page perversely ignores this solution here and through most of his book, except in the first chapter, which is a brilliant and instructive application of the principle of conflation to the Polyphemus episode. See also Lord, *passim,* especially pp. 173–174.

31. On expansion as a feature of epic style, see Whitman, pp. 114–124 and T. B. L. Webster, *From Mycenae to Homer* (New York, 1958), pp. 223–224 and 239–241. On this scene in particular, see Whitman, pp. 121–122. The omen also marks the culmination of another important theme in the *Odyssey:* the development of Telemachus as Odysseus' son and heir.

32. E. V. Rieu, *The Odyssey* (London: Penguin Books, 1946), p. 14 cites the passage as an example of "the tenderness which [Homer] expresses (or rather, in some subtle manner causes us to feel) for all those whom fate or their own follies have afflicted or cast down." Cf. W. B. Stanford, *The Odyssey of Homer* (London, 1958), *ad loc.*

33. The leading exponent of this view was perhaps Gilbert Murray; see, e.g., *The Rise of the Greek Epic* (Oxford, 1907), p. 237. See also C. H. Moore, *The Religious Thought of the Greeks* (Cambridge, Mass., 1916), p. 20, Martin P. Nilsson, *A History of Greek Religion* (Oxford, 1949), pp. 152–153, and C. M. Bowra, *Tradition and Design in the Iliad* (Oxford, 1930), pp. 222–224.

34. Woodhouse, p. 112.

35. For the use of "divine apparatus" in Homer to adorn, clarify, and dramatize the narrative, see S. E. Bassett, *The Poetry of Homer* (Berkeley, 1938), pp. 220–226 and G. M. Calhoun, "Homer's Gods: Prolegomena," *Transactions of the American Philological Association,* LXVIII (1937), 11–25; "Homer's Gods: Myth and Märchen," *American Journal of Philology,* LX (1940), 1–28; "The Divine Entourage in Homer," *American Journal of Philology,* LXI (1941), 257–277.

36. For especially perceptive studies of the meaning of the Homeric gods see E. R. Dodds, *The Greeks and the Irrational* (Berkeley, 1951), pp. 1–27; Walter Otto, *The Homeric Gods* (New York, 1954), *passim;* Whitman, pp. 221–248.

37. Cf. Otto, pp. 189–190. The belief evidently had its roots in Mycenean religion; see Nilsson, p. 155.

38. Cf. C. H. Taylor, "The Obstacles to Odysseus' Return," above.

39. Cf. Stanford, *The Ulysses Theme,* pp. 25–42.

40. Otto, p. 195.

41. An instance of what Freud calls "inversion of affect;" he quotes a striking parallel in which "uncontrollable laughter takes the place of weeping and sobbing at the idea that [the dreamer] has to die" (*Basic Writings,* p. 98).

42. For discussions of the parallels, sometimes striking, between this scene and other folklore and literature (especially the Burnt Njal Saga), see Monro and Stanford *ad loc.* and F. M. Stawell, *Homer and the Iliad* (London, 1909), pp. 226–227. For discussions of the nature of Theoclymenus' vision, which is of a type rare in Greek literature, see W. R. Halliday, *Greek Divination* (London, 1913), p. 75; Edwyn Bevan, *Sibyls and Seers* (London, 1928), pp. 132–152; and Dodds, p. 70.

43. For the architectural problems involved, see the works of Dorothea Gray. Sir John L. Myres, *Homer and His Critics* (London, 1958), pp. 162–170 contains references and a convenient survey of discussions of the Homeric house.

44. The same is true of Athene's intervention in Book Eighteen; see note 6.

45. She herself (23.256 ff.) presses the reluctant Odysseus to tell her of the journey inland foretold to him by Teiresias. She receives in silence his departure to the rest of his estates the morning after their reunion (23. 359 ff.).

46. Woodhouse, pp. 82–83. Harsh, p. 13, remarks that she is willing to set the contest because she is convinced that "only the true Odysseus can string his bow." This was undoubtedly the point of the contest in the original folk tale (cf. Woodhouse, pp. 92–101), but in our *Odyssey* Penelope speaks as if she expected the suitors to be able to accomplish the feat.

47. For divination by lot see also 9.331 ff. and *Iliad* 7.175–183. On the Athenians' use of the lot to choose their magistrates see Plato, Laws 690 C and 759 B-C.

48. On the affiliations between Zeus and Homeric kings, see, e.g., J. A. K. Thomson, *Studies in the Odyssey* (Oxford, 1914), pp. 11–12 and 144–145; compare note 4 above.

49. For the importance of thunder and lightning as omens in classical times, see, e.g., A. B. Cook, *Zeus* (Cambridge, England, 1925), II 4–5 and A. Bouché-Leclercq, *Histoire de la Divination dans l'Antiquité* (Paris, 1879–1882), I 199. For Homer's use of such omens as a device to expedite the narrative, cf. *Iliad* 2.350–353, 8.170 ff. and 9.236–237.

50. *hōs phat' oiomenos laossoon emmen' Athēnēn;* see note 16.

51. Cf. Otto, p. 212.

52. See above, pp. 105–106. Presumably the poet deferred the recognition of husband and wife until after the slaying of the suitors precisely because he wished to explore Penelope's feelings in a leisurely manner, but did not wish to interrupt the tense sequence of action leading to the slaying. Stanford is one of the few critics to appreciate this point; cf. his fine analysis of the relationship between Penelope and Odysseus, *The Ulysses Theme,* pp. 55–59.

53. Cf. Harsh, pp. 5–6.

54. Athene twice enhances the looks of Telemachus (2.12–13 and 17.63–64), once those of Penelope (18.187–197), and once those of Laertes (24.367–370). The motif is used most often of Odysseus: 6.227–235 (where the same simile is used as in 23.156–162), 8.18–23, 16.172–176, and in the passage under discussion. The motif is only incidentally related to the problem of Odysseus' disguise as a beggar, the usual context for discussion of it.

55. Cf. Monro *ad loc.* and Page, pp. 114–115. Lord, p. 176, rather loosely justifies the scene on the grounds of its "ritual significance." It is clear that in other versions the bath led to immediate recognition, but here the poet has kept the motif and ignored its original function. Cf. his use of the motif of Penelope's web. In other versions she must have been forced to marry as soon as she was made to finish the web; in our *Odyssey* the ruse of the web is simply referred to to illustrate Penelope's cleverness, except in 24.147 ff. where the original function survives; see Page, pp. 120–121.

56. Lord, p. 170, erroneously states that Penelope recognizes Odysseus by three signs, the bow, the bath, and the bed. He is therefore surprised (p. 175) that Penelope still has doubts at the beginning of Book Twenty-three. His book is extremely illuminating on the characteristics of oral poetry in general, but his discussion of the Homeric poems is regrettably confused and careless.

57. Cf., for example, Stanford, p. 57, L. A. Post, *From Homer to Menander* (Berkeley, 1951), p. 23, and Mackail, p. 70. Whitman's discussion of the differences between the various recognitions of Odysseus (pp. 300–305) is perceptive.

58. Cf., for example, E. Schwartz, *Odyssee* (Munich, 1924), p. 332, U. von Wilamowitz-Moellendorff, *Homerische Untersuchungen* (Berlin, 1884), p. 71, Monro *ad loc.,* and Mackail, p. 20. M. Van der Valk, *Textual Criticism of the Odyssey* (Leiden, 1949) disposes of the first group of arguments; criticism of Homer's text on the basis of subjective moral judgments is finally falling into the neglect it deserves in any case. But Van der Valk and Harsh, p. 6, in defending the passage, still miss the real point of relevance.

59. It is curiously fashionable to talk as if Penelope really rather liked the suitors; see Woodhouse, p. 201, Stawell, p. 127, and Samuel Butler, *The Authoress of the Odyssey* (London, 1897), p. 130–131. If her faithfulness to Odysseus were really in doubt in our *Odyssey,* then she might have cause to defend her conduct to Odysseus, but it is emphasized throughout that Odysseus trusts her absolutely (cf. 18.281–283).